Add
Value

Add Value

Discover your **VALUES**
find your **WORTH**
gain **FULFILLMENT**
in your **PERSONAL**
and **PROFESSIONAL LIFE**

Mark Carter

WILEY

First published in 2020 by John Wiley & Sons Australia, Ltd
42 McDougall St, Milton Qld 4064

Office also in Melbourne

Typeset in FreightTextProMedium-Regular 11/14 pt by Aptara, India

© John Wiley & Sons Australia, Ltd 2020

The moral rights of the author have been asserted

ISBN: 978-0-730-38402-1

A catalogue record for this book is available from the National Library of Australia

Cover design by Wiley

Cover image © Fokin Ihor/Shutterstock

Internal illustrations: Angela Stefanoff of Goldi Design and Monika Obrist of Refresh Design

10 9 8 7 6 5 4 3 2 1

Disclaimer

Contents

About the author

Mark has over 20 years' experience as a learning and development professional, globally. As a former tour leader and training manager with Contiki Holidays he brings a unique perspective of depth and personal stories to conversations around behavioural sciences, business, value and growth, both personally and professionally.

Mark is an international keynote speaker, trainer and coach. He is the founder of a learning management system for individuals and SMEs. He's a regular contributor to mainstream media including *RendezView*, *News.com*, 2SM/2HD, *Studio 10* and *GQ Australia* in addition to leading business and industry publications like *REB*, *Elite Agent* and *Travel Bulletin*. He is accredited in a variety of recognised leading behavioural profile tools.

In addition to authoring his first book *Ignite Your Potential*, Mark shared an initial overview of his Value Model in his TEDxCasey talk, 'Paws and Effect: How teddy bears increase value perception'.

Born in England, fermented in Scotland, nurtured by Europe and matured through several round-world trips, Mark Carter is a truly global citizen. He now calls Australia (Melbourne) home, where he enjoys the fruits of a sunny lifestyle. Mangoes, after all, don't grow in Edinburgh.

Foreword

We live in an era of hashtag wisdom. Where once we would turn to our elders for guidance and inspiration, we now put influencers on a pedestal, allowing them to dust off and churn out tired old clichés and motivational one-liners that attempt to capture the complexities of life into hashtag-sized snacks for the masses. *Warning:* If this is what you are looking for, it may be a good time to put this book down and log onto Facebook.

Feeling challenged? #nevergiveup

Feeling nostalgic? #tbt

Feeling grateful? #blessed

Need attention? #humblebrag

The problem with these cute little catchphrases is that they inevitably fall short of offering any true insight or universal truth. They simply become shortcuts to superficial expression and worse still, have the potential to feed your delusions about life and actually hide the truth from you. Buddhism suggests the path to enlightenment as being able to journey deep within yourself to shatter false beliefs and behavioural habits. The more we attempt to succinctly define truth with any amount of brevity, the further we move from our ability to understand its true meaning.

This is why so many people struggle to establish a true connection with others: they lack the narrative to articulate emotions through words.

In his book *The Prophet*, Kahlil Gibran wrote:

> Your hearts know in silence the secrets of the days and the nights. But your ears thirst for the sound of your heart's knowledge. You would know in words that which you have always known in thought. You would touch with your fingers the naked body of your dreams.

In this beautifully crafted prose, Gibran suggests that we are all inherently born with self-knowledge. We just need to tap into its truth. And this understanding of self has never been more relevant than now, as we find ourselves on the verge of a new era in artificial intelligence. Very quickly, machines are starting to replace the need for us to complete mundane tasks, but they can never replace the emotional aptitude required for us to live a fulfilled life. Industry 4.0 will inevitably increase the importance and need for self-awareness, self-regulation, empathy and social skills.

I first met Mark during the curation process for TEDxCasey. While I was initially enamoured by his contagious enthusiasm and high-octane presence, I soon discovered that it was his understanding of people and his unique style of contextual storytelling that truly allowed him to engage with others to awaken and expand consciousness. A modern day shaman, if you will.

In this book, Mark takes storytelling to a new level by deep diving into the world of 'value' using concepts from some of our greatest thought leaders and lessons from his own unique journey. I would encourage you to find your own little corner of the universe and create an environment that will allow you to read, absorb and find your own meaning. This book is the deep dive we all need to go beyond the superficial presented to us in our daily lives.

In the end, your journey must be defined on your own terms. Use this book as a compass for your own path and create a world that is truly yours. #happyreading

Chris Hall
Entrepreneur and startup guru

Acknowledgements

Thanks to all at TEDxCasey and friends who turned up to support the event. To Viki, Mama Bear, for connecting Lucy; in turn Chris, Sandra and all at Wiley who supported the completion of this book.

TTI Success Insights: among my preferred instruments of choice when consulting behavioural sciences.

Contiki colleagues and clients: some of my longest standing friends and allies. Ten years in the laboratory of 13-metre-long tour coaches turns out among the best petri dish experiments for insights into human behaviour! Not to mention the rich tapestry of history, culture and traditions one is exposed to.

Thanks Chris for the foreword and collaborations past, present and future. Carter-Hall podcasts are going to be fun Hawkman!

For my immediate family: Nick and Judy, John and Nova, Dad, Connor, Ross, Paul and Sally, and Frances. Regardless the distance, space or time you remain in my own Dunbar's number! Thanks too, Mum (going above and beyond motherly duties, turning four decades' experience as a librarian into a role as informal editor!).

To my agents (all at ICMI), clients, collaborators, friends and supporters: there are far too many kind souls, including you as a reader, who support my work. I look forward to our paths crossing at a live event. As an eager cross-legged listener, if you hear or see the author in the storytelling speaker, we've done well.

As a special thanks, you can unlock secret content in my academy. Complimentary registration and login buttons are on my website www.markcarter.com.au

Bespoke Code: ADDVALUE

I'd also like to pay homage to all traditional custodians of Australia. The day I landed here, in 2002, after being a nomad for so many years, I had a strong sense that Australia was to be my home base. Whilst it took 3 months tracking down all necessary paperwork, I was granted my initial residence visa (temporary) within 10 days of lodging the application. I feel privileged to be adopted by a country with, likely, the oldest continual culture. An aboriginal philosophy on knowledge and learning says 'the more you know the less you need.' In a world frequently driven by materialism and consumption this is a sound reminder. You are your greatest tool of value.

It's perhaps serendipitous, strange or fortunate, that timing means as we send this book to print we are feeling the impact globally of COVID19, coronavirus. With it comes generosity and selflessness along with their counterparts, opportunism and selfishness. Fear is the energy that contracts. Love is the energy that expands. Even amid the experience of short periods of social distancing we can use the opportunity to be more connected. Every life event is an opportunity to choose love…and add value.

Introduction

'Define *value* for me.'

I first asked this question almost two decades ago.

I was coaching Chris, who had been successful in business. As a manager he was struggling with coaching and leading a team of others to achieve similar results.

He paused before answering, slightly puzzled.

'I've never really thought about it.'

This struck me as curious for two reasons. The first is he clearly knew how to build or demonstrate value (in a client's sense anyway) given his prior results. The second struck me as somewhat stranger. Surely the concept of value (in business) is an important synergy: like the engine to a car. Without one you're left with an empty decorative shell.

After more serious pause and thought, Chris added with uncertainty, 'It's what people are willing to pay for. Isn't it?'

I continued to search with further open-ended probing.

'Is it? Is that all of it? What else is there? What else might others consider?'

No matter how versatile his offerings, Chris still felt a comprehensive, succinct view of value remained elusive despite the running tally of valid piecemeal definitions building up like a smorgasbord. Not because I'd told him any of his answers were right or wrong. They all had merit.

Chris, like virtually everyone else I've asked since, intuitively knew there's more to 'value'. They just can't quite put their finger on it.

So what is 'value'?

In business, value is commonly accepted as a crucial component of the customer equation. We've even given it a label: value proposition. If you don't provide value, there's no reason you'll land or keep a client.

That's partially why Chris's initial answer leaped straight to the idea of 'what someone is willing to pay for something'. It's a very narrow, bottom-line-minded viewpoint. Not all decisions are based on return on investment, or 'show me the money!'

That's part of the reason I've discovered people have to dig deeper to consider what value really means to them. Value has become so linked to commercial metrics and measures of success that we frequently miss what may prove to be an even greater treasure, even for those corporate clients with shareholders to please and profit-and-loss sheets to reconcile.

You've no doubt heard the mantra 'adding value', whether it be in relation to adding real value in business or sustaining quality relationships in our personal lives. We all look at our world differently, so to assume value and quality are perceived by others the same way we perceive them can limit our ability to truly connect with others. In business, it can limit our ability to effectively communicate and connect with clients or collaborators.

If you inspect value more closely, what also becomes crystal clear is that it underpins an important place in every part of our lives: personal bonds, an ability to influence communities or even legacies we may leave behind. Value permeates every nook and cranny in life. If a human being were a land mass, then value would be a combination of the existing wells that rise within, or the ocean that surrounds and continually massages it in tides, serving to nourish and enrich its potential.

This is why I found it all the more curious that during an extensive, continued quest it was surprisingly rare to find anyone with absolute clarity or conviction of the total meaning of value. It was far more common to find ambiguity and sometimes confusion in responses—'I've never really thought about it' and 'Ummm ...' being two of the more typical.

In those early days I also turned to many gospels of knowledge as a part of my inquisitiveness including white papers, opinion pieces and the *Oxford English Dictionary*. Even this greatest testament of tuition, established for the sole purpose of clarity in definition, yields a variety of subjective short answers, some similar to those offered by respondents.

All of which leads to the somewhat accurate conclusion that the regard that something is held to deserve—its importance, its worth or usefulness, its value—is linked to *perception*.

Individuals have a tendency to perceive and assume value through specific, often favoured, filters. The risk with this preferential default approach means we may alienate, or not as easily align with, others. A further inability to pick up on subtle clues when approaching situations habitually means we may completely miss the value mark. Which beckons the questions:

- What are any of those perceptions based on?
- What's the difference between my own and others' impressions?
- What motivates my choices or notions of value?

And perhaps the most powerful question (for your professional or personal life):

- What motivates the sensation in others?

Human behaviour

Values are an integral part of addressing human behaviour because a person's thoughts translated into actions are a direct representation — a strong statement — of what they believe in and prioritise. Human behaviour has been studied for many centuries: from Hippocrates, who developed a theory that moods, emotions and behaviour had an impact on the essential bodily fluids; to Leonardo da Vinci, who expanded previous personality models to incorporate layers that many people would consider pseudo-science (herbalism, astrology and the like); to the modern-day Myers–Briggs Type Indicator® personality test, which makes the theory of Swiss psychiatrist Carl Jung's eight profile types comprehensible and useful in people's lives. Essentially, Jung's theory was that seemingly random behaviour can be a result of basic differences in the way people use their perception and judgement.

It's elemental

In the 5th century BCE, the philosopher Empedocles proposed the classical theory that there are four fundamental elements present in all matter. We know these classical elements as earth, air, fire and water. In modern times they may also be referenced respectively as solids, gas, plasma and liquids.

A century later, the Ancient Greek alchemist of philosophy, Aristotle (384–322 BCE), surmised all things were a combination of both matter and form and theorised a correlation between potentiality and actuality.

Aristotle's burning log

Aristotle burned a log to show how the four classical elements coexist within all matter to differing proportions:

- earth/solids are the charcoal and ash as they fall
- air/gas is released through smoke, rising quickly
- fire/plasma are the flames rising quickly
- water/liquid bubbles out and also falls.

Experimenting with these elements, Aristotle also differentiated a fifth element, one that allowed for perfection or movements of more otherworldly, divine objects such as the heavens, planets and stars. This elusive element later became known as 'aether'.

In a separate yet related concept, Aristotle proposed a story for causality — the *why* of something. The simple way to look at it is that everything made from any or all of the classical elements may take its ultimate form through an active journey of four causes, or layers. Together these four layers answer the *why* of something.

The Value Model

Aristotle's model is a beautiful, simple framework with which to package the philosophy of value. So it made sense to me that I should leverage some of Aristotle's inspiration when structuring a philosophical model on how to add, create and appreciate value — all with the aim of helping people be authentic and connect with others.

If you were to ask hundreds of people to define 'value' you'd get hundreds of different answers. I know, because I've done it. However, within these definitions are core patterns with which to neatly package a more digestible explanation that can be leveraged with powerful purpose.

The value model I introduce and explore in this book is designed to prepare you to manage the challenges of today and tomorrow—both business and personal—by tapping into a complete sense of your values.

Just as Aristotle's five elements each have four causes, the five values that make up the Value Model each have four layers that underpin them.

These five values—personal, tangible, emotional, service and relationship (more on these shortly)—are the subject matter of chapters 1 to 5 of this book (the 'value' chapters).

As with Aristotelian deductive reasoning, none of the Value Model's five values satisfactorily lives in isolation.

We may all have strong preferences towards certain values and behaviours, yet they all coexist to varying degrees within everyone's individual perception.

Our inclinations vary depending on situational considerations —personal and professional life being obvious ones. The priority or importance given to something is another. Plus, our underlying values, or value system, play a critical part. It's my hope that reading this book will help you remove any biases or habitual filters with which you may view our world in order to elevate both connection and perception of value using simple ideas such as storytelling.

And these perceptions don't remain static or set in stone. Just like the motion of the all-magic aether, the continual journey and circle of life entails navigating situations and influences from external factors that may affect our preferences of value.

As you devour or absorb the intricacies of the Value Model, make sure to pause and ponder where you may be firmly rooted, or consider how you might adapt. A strong stance to adopt, which

I'll dive into in chapter 6, is to embody as many, if not all, of the values by default. Your life and the lives of others will be all the richer, fuller and more rewarding for it because the ideas in each component of the Value Model, when applied with conscious awareness and effort, will improve your ability to connect with others, both personally and professionally.

I've included in each 'value' chapter some tips and ideas I call 'self-reflEQtions'—because I've come to realise, the more I work in the field of human behaviour, that it is the soft skills and human skills associated with EQ that become ever more important. The purpose of the self-reflEQtions is to provoke initial thoughts and apply emotional intelligence for each value. You'll find additional extended ones in supporting content online at portal.markcarter.com.au (use the bespoke code 'ADDVALUE' when setting up your free profile).

Human beings are onions!

It is not the purpose of this book to act as a bible for behavioural models or psychoanalysis tools. It is to paint a context of where they have come from and why they are important to perceptions of the world around us, including value. In the same way science continues to evolve, so do people and our understanding of human behaviour. Every year additional studies, research papers and generally accepted ideas are released in relation to personality, traits and behaviours. While you can't package any individual one neatly into a single box, many of these models have merit. There are dozens of commonly accepted behavioural profiling tools. The more you're exposed to, the easier it is to see glaringly obvious commonalities. They help us better understand ourselves and others. They help explain why some things may be prioritised by us or others. There are times people perceive things so differently, or their behaviour is so foreign, we're left wondering if we're really all from the same planet! So what are these tools objectively looking at or measuring?

This is where an expanded awareness of neuroscience and the human brain come into play. Behavioural tools help us unravel—like the layers of an onion—different aspects of this journey and existence we call being human: the manner with which we gather or take in information and perceive our environment; how we then compute, analyse or make sense of that data; the method by which we come to conclusions or decisions; and the manner in which we communicate, relate and deal with our external world.

Among these layers (which are also referred to as causes, dichotomies, traits and metrics in chapters 1 to 5) we can rip into the fabrics that weave our perceptions of value, values and self-worth.

The five values

The Value Model is designed to provide context and practical, bite-sized understandings that will inspire you to discover possibilities in approaching your world differently.

As I briefly touched on, the five overarching values are:

1. *Relationship value:* Quality relationships with others is a significant aspect of our life. No-one is designed to be an island. Relationships that, like fire, offer warmth are the ones we treasure most.

2. *Service value:* We also have a synergy with others in giving and receiving service. Being of service to others is an airborne elixir that allows the world to harmoniously evolve.

3. *Emotional value:* We're all driven by emotions. Our mental states act like an internal compass to help us make a decision. Water is a universal symbol representing our emotional states or moods.

4. *Tangible value:* Individuals appreciate the tangible exchange of measurable goods or services. Tangible transactions, then, are very grounded, like earth, allowing us to benchmark and measure our world.

5. *Personal value:* This is the special value in my Value Model. It is people—all individuals—who give meaning to the other four values and truly bring them to life.

Our journey of discovering the Value Model begins with the personal value—that is, with understanding people better. In the same way that Aristotle saw the aether as being, somewhat, otherworld, there are times when we deal with others and we're left wondering: Are we really all from the same planet?

1

Personal value

Identifying your *how, why, do* and *who*

My deep fascination with the nature of people began while working for Contiki Holidays as a leader and Training & Development Manager across Europe. I often joke that it was the best live laboratory one could wish for! Akin, somewhat, to being inside a 13-metre-long petri dish reality experiment of human behaviour, made more fascinating by the dynamics of individuality and environment playing out.

Imagine it. You have a group of 50 young adults, aged between 18 and 35, from every corner of the globe. Already you have a melting pot of cultures, people brought up with different influences (family and country two of these) as a starting point. Add to this a variety of professions, attitudes and of course what we're beginning to explore here, personality types. It's the perfect forum for observing people and mastering skills relative to human behaviour. If you're paying attention that is! All guests were encouraged to complete a feedback form at the end of their tour—in fact it was imperative. The corporate office held high expectations of consistently great feedback. If road crew received unfavourable feedback they'd be at risk of having their contract payment docked.

In fact so much was the pressure that at one point there was a 'black market' for blank feedback forms. Some tour leaders may, if they felt members of their group had given them an unruly slating, be inclined to 'doctor' a new version.

I never saw the point in doctoring or amending those forms. I'm not perfect. I don't claim to be. I've never been. It's better to be open to learning from perceptions from others rather than run or hide. That said, I also understand why some peers might be tempted.

Yet even within an environment that provided every individual the rich rewards and valuable experiences we associate with exploring cultures, some people were never happy. Then, when asked for written feedback, all they could muster up was negative, often mundane, complaints: hotel rooms were too small; music choices on long journeys were crap; or any number of fairly minor criticisms. They might also attack the decisions or behaviour of their road crew (sometimes with just cause) often times without full consideration. When you're leading groups of people, including 50 tourists, around multiple countries with so many considerations of logistics, risk, compliance and personalities, it's impossible to appease or please everyone all the time.

I recall after one of my first tours several people wrote similar feedback. Something along the lines of 'Mark's a great guy, but he shows favouritism'.

When asked about it by the office, I reflected and pondered a better question. What was I doing that made some people think or feel I was showing favouritism? The answer struck me like a lightning bolt. I'm naturally an outgoing, energetic person, drawn to banter and fun. Back then, with the hindrance of youth and far less wisdom, even more so! So, doing the rounds on those longer travel days, with hours spent on the coach, I'd find myself talking longer with people like me: somewhat extroverted, a little cheeky and playful. I may not have been spending as long or been as boisterous or bold with the reserved passengers, who were naturally a little more quiet despite attempts to encourage them from their shells. In my mind, giving them a little peace was meant respectfully so as not to disturb them. They were interpreting this as preferential treatment.

I subsequently learned to pre-empt this situation. I'd call it out on the first day of my tours. After learning everyone's names I'd let them know they all had access to my available time equally. All they needed to do was ask. I never had feedback about showing favouritism again.

Personal value in a nutshell

Within the realm of personal value we can identify four layers:

1. Preference: *how* we function
2. Motivation: finding your *why*
3. Intelligence — IQ & EQ: your ability to *do*
4. Everything else: *who* am I?

Let's discover the intricacies of each of these personal value layers so that you can leverage your strengths, identify your motivation, apply EQ with an open mindset and look for clues in others.

1. Preference: *how* we function

My 'aha' moment at Contiki is one simple example amid thousands concerning the dynamics of *how* people prefer to function. Working in that environment for years, I built my own playbook for behavioural sciences for the purpose of harmonising groups, resolving conflict, selling excursions and even problem solving some pretty significant or severe crises. Later, when undertaking multiple accreditations and qualifications, I found the courses instantly recognisable.

The initial surface of personal value perception to peel back is the outer one we see and interact with—it's simply how people prefer to function. When you're attentive, you start to see clues to the mix of people's preferences.

Profiling tools are not designed to put people in boxes or give them labels. And no single one explains the sophistication or complexity of individuality. What they are great for is to begin to hone in on clues. No-one lives in a single area, a single label. You may find some resonate more strongly than others or notice certain traits more clearly than others in the people around you. These help indicate some of the tendencies or preferences of *how* we like to function. They also have an impact on the worldly perception of value or worth.

American psychologist, lawyer and inventor William Moulton Marston published a paper in 1928 entitled 'Emotions of normal people', in which he proposed that human behaviour was, in part, influenced by whether what the person perceived of their environment was favourable or not. He observed a strong connection between emotion and blood pressure and is credited with inventing systolic blood pressure testing, an integral component of the polygraph lie-detector tests. There have been suggestions his work was based on lessons from his wife Elizabeth. He noted that 'when she got mad or excited, her blood pressure seemed to climb'.

In his paper, Marston laid out theories and concepts that became the basis of DISC theory, which comprises a set of profiling tools that categorise people according to four personality types:

- Dominance produces activity in an antagonistic environment: dominant people are results driven individuals who may be perceived by others as ambitious, driving and decisive.

- Influence produces activity in a favourable environment: influencers are outgoing, warm, expressive individuals who have a tendency to give trust more openly.

- Steadiness produces passivity in a favourable environment: steady people value consistency and prefer quality over quantity. They're naturally more patient, predictable, empathetic and are good listeners.

- Compliance produces passivity in an antagonistic environment: compliant people appreciate the provision of procedures, constraints, rules and a standard playbook of regulations. They tend to be detailed, precise, careful and systematic.

What to do with the how

We have a tendency to act out and display our preferences in everything we do. Let's take something as simple as organising a picnic.

Some among us (let's go high Influence preference) when planning that outing will tend to leave things to the last minute. They'd be less aware of holidays that might interfere with such plans. You're more likely to receive an invite days out or spontaneously far closer to time rather than a month in advance. They'll invite whoever springs to mind, unaware or oblivious as to whether riffs among groups of friends might prove disruptive on the day. They'll choose a fun location and aren't really thinking about where every individual may be coming from. You'll be asked to bring food, drinks and perhaps some games. On the day they'll arrive enthusiastic, even if a little late and disorganised, for their own event.

Others among us who are their friends (let's go high Compliance preference) will receive the aforementioned invitation and have an initial reaction of WTF! Or they may have a slight panic attack, a minor bout of anxiety, on behalf of their organising friend. You'll know these souls because they're the ones who kindly phone or write back with the tagline 'Mark, thanks for the invite. I'm sure it will be fun. I've just got a few questions'. Questions along the lines of: Where exactly are we meeting in that grassy area in the park? What if it's raining? You do know that Oliver and Lisa aren't talking right now, so maybe not such a good idea to have them both there until they patch things up? By the way Mark, what should I, or anyone else bring? If we don't write a list we're likely to end up with multiple chickens and not enough salads, surely, aren't we? Oh, one last thing Mark, I know you don't have children but next time you may want to consider doing this a month or so later when the school holidays are on. This will be far easier for many of us.

In a different scenario, imagine after a great week at work a decision is made to go for team drinks. Some (let's go high Dominance preference) will march straight out the door leading the way to the nearest decent bar, especially when they know happy hour is just about to start. Others from the group (let's go with high Steadiness preference) will see the aforementioned results-driven colleague/friend and holler out to them, 'Hey, Ryan! Who died and made you commander in chief?' indicating with a circular hand motion the entire group. They'd likely then add 'We haven't talked about it yet. We may want to go somewhere else!'

They will then invite a huddle—a group discussion—ensuring input is heard from everyone.

Meanwhile Ryan, now 30 metres ahead and moonwalking subtly backwards Michael Jackson style in the direction of the obvious establishment of choice, turns back to the gang. He spanks the palm of his hand on his forehead in despair while hollering a friendly, yet short and curt reply. 'What are you on about! We're right here aren't we? We're wasting time and happy hour anywhere will be done by the time you lot finish talking about it!'

We're all individuals

We are who we are. It's jungle law (kind of)! Think about it like this. A lion is a lion, you see. A lion wants to roam the plains hunting wildebeest, taking long naps, not fussed by others between those mealtimes. Because that's what a lion likes to do. A lion doesn't want to swing in trees playing with monkeys or splash around in the water with baby elephants thank you very much.

If you're inclined towards analytics and detail, you're going to value data.

If you've a tendency to big picture or ideas, you'll value freedom to explore.

If you're results driven, you'll appreciate the value of getting shit done.

If you have an inclination towards harmony, conversations with others are of high worth.

As accredited profiling tools—including my favourite instruments from TTI Insights Success—stipulate, these preferences are *not*, I repeat *not*:

- a measure or indication of skill
- a measure of education or training
- a benchmark or measure of a person's intelligence
- an indicator of someone's underlying values.

We'll get to some of those in the other layers of personal value. A preference is simply that. One person may be drawn to view big-picture thinking with a desire to break from the rules. Yet in doing so they may be more skilled than others who know the rules well.

These initial ideas help identify a practical road map for improving the value and quality of such things as communication, collaboration or minimising conflict with others.

Another nuance of human behaviour is that so often we may not appreciate our own value, not realising the worth of what we bring to the table. When we get caught in a game of comparison with others we may devalue ourselves. All individuals have unique gifts of value to share with the world, regardless of the weighting of those preferences. These predilections may lend themselves to a natural set of skills or gifts in addition to Achilles heels. Table 1.1 presents a snapshot of what I mean.

Table 1.1: Potential strengths and cautions of tendencies

Strengths	Cautions
Dominant tendency	
Direct candid communication	Too blunt or cold
Streamlines efficiently	Shoots down others' ideas
Evaluates risk swiftly	Won't consider all perspectives
Time conscious	Decisions at the expense of collaboration
Systematic, organised approach	Little patience for reasoning
Influence tendency	
Inspiring, engaging communication	Talks too much or over the top
Blue sky thinking, creative ideas	Over-promises or takes on too much
Anticipates opportunities	Misses crucial information required
Pivots and adapts quickly	Innovates at the expense of logic
Lifts energy or inspires others	Goes off on left field tangents
Steadiness tendency	
Empathetic, listening, communicative	Shies from difficult conversations
Builds strong relationships	Side-tracked in conversations

Consolidates trust and satisfaction	Collaborates at the expense of decisions
Anticipates others' expectations	Procrastinates or loses pace
Compliance tendency	
In-depth evidenced communication	Long-winded excessive information
Establishes processes and systems	May miss the big picture or vision
Demonstrates ROI	Slow to momentum or to adapt
Identifies trends in the data patterns	Safe logic at the expense of innovation
Fulfills compliance, mitigates risks	Overthinks

I'd emphasise that an inclination towards any skill doesn't guarantee being more masterful. Someone who considers their creative talents meagre, believing their strength lies in mechanics and details, may yield a harvest of fruitful innovation, even in comparison with the day-dreaming individual with a tendency towards that trait.

Conversely, one who seems to think in big colourful pictures with little patience or inclination for administrative spreadsheets may find their skill for detail, when applied, equal or even greater than the person preferring solitary work in the quest for quantitative data and research.

And so ...

As a way of wrapping up the *how*, or first layer, of personal value, let's simplify the four DISC personality types into two streams of practical, useable observations by way of three examples.

In general conversations there are two types of people:

- *those who listen*—they don't interrupt or talk over the top of others. They tend to internalise their viewpoint to gain clarity before speaking aloud to share their answer. This can be after a short, or even somewhat longer, period of silence. For those who don't function this way, that quiet equates to feeling like a fortnight and they succumb to the temptation to fill the void with more noise! In doing so, the silent partner, who was on the verge of giving you a thoughtful answer, is now forced back to the beginning of the thinking process to ponder the new question posed, the danger then being they never really get the time or space required and cutting them off means missing their valuable inputs.

- *those who talk*—including talking over the top of others (a slightly rude habit to be mindful of!). They externalise aloud, in draft, downloading all their thoughts and viewpoints as though tipping out all the Lego bricks. The conversation, its shape shifting like sand dunes, is mined as they go, building clarity from the chatter. Some people, listening to the roving, adapting, seemingly random soliloquy may wonder 'Do we really need to hear all of this?' The answer is yes, as it's in the speaking aloud that clarity comes. To gag the outpour is to damn their wisdom.

So which way is better? They both are equal, as each method allows the individual to digest information and share viewpoints. We can be more mindful and patient with each other.

In conflict there are two types of people:

- *those requiring time-out to mull things over*—they find calm in the quiet space left by your absence and so for a period it's best to leave them be. For others, who don't operate this way, it may prove difficult to understand or identify with them. Rather, they want to keep pressing a resolution without realising the more you're in the other party's face the further away you drive them. Respect the space, acknowledge the other party requires time-out, then simply ask that they come back to you as soon as they can, knowing your own mind will likely be stuck in overthinking loops in the meantime.

- *those who want to talk about it right now*—they say, 'we're already together, in discussion, so let's just hammer it out'. There's no need for space apart or long silences. Again, you see the contrast. For those requiring a pause this may seem exceptionally intense, without realising how much the time-out plays on the other party's mind. Perhaps again we can learn to respect the other, acknowledging you know the discussion is important, and give a promise to then come back as soon as you're ready. The key here is to follow through on the promise and not extend longer silences than necessary or just cut people off and ghost.

Again, neither method is more correct or better than the other.

As a final example, in general commitments and projects there are also two types of people:

- *those who break a task down, step-by-step, into equal amounts*—they will likely work at a steady pace with regular updates to follow through as promised and complete the commitment either ahead of or right on time.

- *those whose preference would be to potentially put it on ice until the commitment becomes more pressing or urgent*—the majority of activity required ramps up in the final few days with little updates along the way. They then slide in, ahead of or on time, to hit a home run, the reason being that this self-induced pressure is where their magic happens.

Which method is correct? Well, hopefully you get a sense now that they both are. Provided commitments are met to standard, and on time, does it really matter?

To judge less and show greater patience and appreciation for *how* others prefer to function can reduce so much tension and conflict. If we make an effort in only a few adaptations, we needn't change who we are to add value to our external world.

How people prefer to function is not a stand-alone indicator or explanation of perception of value, values or even self-worth. This outer layer may be accentuated or tethered when working in conjunction with the other layers of the 'human onion'. For example, *how* people function doesn't automatically translate or explain *why*.

2. Motivation: finding your *why*

To highlight how ingrained the second layer of our personal value is within us all, let's consider for a moment the pre-historic alpha hunter and the modern-day equivalent.

(Wo)man returns to the cave empty-handed. Whereas this was once a disaster meaning hunger or angst for the tribe, it's now not so much of a strain as the spoils to tackle these days are salaries with a regular pay cheque, not the claws of rampant, angry prey.

Upon entering the cave, now called a house, (wo)man dumps their weapons, these days a laptop and gym bag, in the corner. Hungry, after a long day battling a variety of beasts (these days a mixed bag of human personality types, some of them weirdos), (wo)man grunts as they swing open the Fisher & Paykel fridge door.

Peering inside with mouth-watering curiosity, they begin rummaging through the leftovers—you know, foil-covered plates with the food from Sunday, Saturday or even the Thursday before this manic Monday.

Uninspired by dried remains of roast dinners or withered, hardened pasta they begin to rifle other mediocre offerings, the trophies available for end-of-the-month prior to payday.

There's a quarter of a carton of milk, only just out of date. The last scrapings in the Vegemite jar prove difficult to procure even with the help of a butter knife. And anyway the last of the lavosh is corners and crumbs from broken biscuits left from a prior late night snack attack of the munchies.

The final straw is seeing the tomato sauce bottle top, firm like cement from the excess of prior squeezing. It's going to take more than Gordon Ramsay inspiration to pull anything edible together with this sad-looking lot. So a grunt turns to 'f*ck it' as (wo)man decides it's time to go hunting and replenish the stock.

Of course, this no longer means an existence of sitting silently alert for hours in bushes wondering where the next meal may come from. It also no longer requires the efforts of co-hunters. In fact, gathering these days as a group inevitably leads to bickering rather than a unified approach. Decision made, (wo)man heads off alone on a mission straight to the rich hunting ground known as the shops.

They know this terrain so well: the exact order of aisles to walk down in order to hunt and gather basic supplies for the next couple of weeks. So they're in and out like a ninja. They return to the cave, throw out the old, and load up with the new stocks. Now they can put their feet up to enjoy some kind of unreal reality with a tray full of goodies resting on their belly as a minor feast after another successful hunt.

There are three primary drivers for motivation. This, my friends, is a rudimentary summary of the first type of motivation—biological—which has barely changed in thousands of years. (We'll get to the other two—extrinsic motivation and intrinsic motivation—shortly.)

In the days of our earliest ancestors (long before Aristotle said 'at his best, man is the noblest of all animals, separated from law and justice he is the worst') our motivations—our *why*—were very simple: survive and propagate.

If you were hungry, you'd be driven to find food and eat. If you were thirsty, you'd drink. If you felt fear, you'd run away to fight another day.

Biological motivation is inherent in our DNA. We find ourselves driven to follow these impulses as a natural part of survival, to reproduce and to evolve. The 'body clock' kicks in after seeing one too many cute munchkins or reaching a certain stage of life where procreation feels almost necessary. The fight-or-flight mechanism we reach for is still hardwired in our brains, although the manner with which we leverage the response has changed.

There are many people who find that motivation is fluff or pseudoscience. Thinking about our drive in relation to satiating biological desires is a great start to breaking down the different sorts of drive that exist.

From biological needs to the other drivers

Abraham Maslow (1908–1970) was raised in New York during a period of racism and prejudices, not only in the broader external world but also within his own home. Internally, Maslow said he didn't have the type of strong bond other progeny have with their parents: 'Since my mother is the type that's called schizophrenogenic in literature—she's the one who makes crazy people, crazy children—I was awfully curious to find out why I didn't go insane'.

Maslow 'reacted' against her values and views. He saw his mother as selfish, unloving, self-serving, prejudiced (especially against people of colour) and with a closed mind to life, saying anyone who disagreed with her was wrong.

As a professor of psychology, Maslow cultivated an interest in human health and fulfillment based on needs in a priority order.

His model, released in 1943 under the title 'A Theory of Human Motivation' became better known as 'Maslow's Hierarchy of Needs'.

As a humanistic psychologist, Maslow believed people had an inherent drive towards 'self-actualisation', a desire, if you will, to fully realise their own potential, fulfillment, capabilities and creativities—that is, their deeper intrinsic motivation. Maslow was somewhat critical of Sigmund Freud's works. 'It is as if Freud supplied us the sick half of psychology and we must now fill it out with the healthy half'.

Maslow's theory was illustrated in a five-stage pyramid. As individuals' most pressing needs were fulfilled, they'd give attention to the next level and so on: beginning at the bottom running to the peak of the pyramid.

1. At the base of the pyramid are our basic or physiological needs: breathing, food, water, sleep, reproduction, homeostasis, excretion.

2. The second level consists of safety needs: security, order and stability: security of body, employment, resources, morality, family, health, property.

These first two steps are related to the basic physical survival—fight-or-flight—of an individual. Maslow's theory stated that once the boxes for nutrition, shelter and safety have been ticked an individual becomes motivated to accomplish more. But until our base needs have been taken care of it's hard to tap into the higher levels of self-actualisation.

3. The third level is identified as love and belonging: friendship, family and sexual intimacy.

Once an individual has got themselves together, taking care of business as it were, they are ready to share themselves with others.

4. The fourth level is the esteem level: self-esteem, confidence, achievement, respect of others, respect by others.

These first four levels became known as 'deficit needs', meaning if you didn't have enough in the tank you'd be left discontent and wanting. But once these deficit needs were mostly fulfilled contentment would follow. At this point individuals began to explore the need for harmony. Feeling a sense of harmony and contentment, individuals would then explore 'self-actualisation' to reach their full potential and accomplish goals.

So, order, or beauty, was the path to the fifth level.

5. The top of the pyramid is labelled the 'need for self-actualisation': morality, creativity, spontaneity, problem solving, lack of prejudice, acceptance of facts.

Maslow's term 'metamotivated'—becoming everything one is capable of becoming—sums up the context of self-actualisation. Perhaps fuelled by experiences with his own mother, he observed its nature was individual—and indeed some people seem to achieve self-actualisation via a 'healthy narcissism'.

Maslow's model has come increasingly under scrutiny and fire from a 'scientific' standpoint, primarily due to his research methods. He included arguably subjective biographical analysis and lacked somewhat the empirical evidence required.

That said, we see there are some common-sense truths to the concepts and theories of personal drive. It's not as obvious to focus on others if you're living in poverty or on the breadline yourself. You're not necessarily going to feel the love if you're being bullied, rejected or disrespected by others. If you're lacking self-confidence, you may be less inclined to drive towards igniting potential.

So in this sense Maslow's work is worthy of fuelling self-reflection relating to *why* you do things as part of the 'science' of motivation.

Extrinsic and intrinsic drivers expanded

In the 1960s, social psychologist Douglas McGregor created a recognisable theory for motivation based on how managers view their people. His is the single fundamental model that really helps highlight the difference between extrinsic and intrinsic motivation. He came up with two distinctly different theories to explain how their beliefs about what motivates them can affect their management style. He called these Theory X and Theory Y.

Theory X

This theory worked on the assumption that individuals have little ambition and that some aren't particularly goal oriented and work purely for self-interest and essentials. McGregor contended that the management style to adopt in this situation in order to maximise efficiency and results had to be hands on.

In order to motivate individuals Theory X proposed using rewards and/or punishment. These external, extrinsic drivers, regardless of whether they were good or bad, served as fuel to ignite the human spirit and potential.

Within Theory X was space for both a hard- and a soft-manner approach. We know of course the hard one as being micro-management: full on, hands on, being the watchful eye and even at times including intimidation. The caution here was that using this approach may foster hostility and negativity within an environment and risked reducing an individual's self-worth.

A softer, more lenient version has more relevant validity. Some people only find their mojo when impacted by external factors. Used wisely, this axis of reward or punishment might be a path to help ignite self-motivation. There is a downside, however. Building an environment where individuals become reliant on rewards risks fostering a sense of entitlement, stretching over estimations of one's own worth or capabilities and even low outputs without benefit or remuneration.

Theory Y

This premise held the view that individuals were more inclined to take responsibility and accountability for all their results, thereby requiring less supervision.

This internal desire, being like Maslow's highest pyramid step of self-actualisation, drives people to strive to reach their full potential or to perform at their very best, fuelled from a deeper burning fire within: an internal or intrinsic motivation.

Like Maslow, McGregor believed the path to self-actualisation was more fulfilling and delivered the greater reward. His model is perhaps simpler to remember and absorb than Maslow's, but together these models are rooted in motivation theory.

Those of you who read motivational books may also recognise Theory X and Theory Y packaged slightly differently in the work of Daniel Pink, author of *Drive*.

Happiness and motivation

In the 2011 documentary *Happy*—directed, written and co-produced by Roko Belic, who interviewed people in 14 different countries for the documentary—further context helps us differentiate intrinsic and extrinsic motivation or goals. In some ways these views lend kudos to support common-sense factors within Maslow's model.

Daniel Gilbert, PhD and author of *Stumbling on Happiness*, says 'Anybody who says money can't buy happiness has never met someone who lives in a cardboard box under a bridge'. He adds, 'But anybody who tells you money buys happiness has never met a very rich person'.

In other words, anyone living in poverty has the possibility of being elevated to middle-class status with money; however, beyond that money makes little difference.

Many individuals, no matter the wealth, resources or material goods they can access, learn to adapt and live within, to the full extent, the new level of means and still crave a desire for more.

So in order to find happiness the delineation between external (extrinsic) and internal (intrinsic) motivation helps us find a path to being 'happy'.

A contemporary view of extrinsic and intrinsic motivation

Extrinsic goals include reward or praise, but also apply to the accumulation of 'stuff', primarily:

- money and financial success
- image and looking good
- status and popularity.

Conversely, intrinsic goals are psychological needs geared towards *being* more rather than *having* more. The primary types of fulfillment are inherently satisfying in and of themselves:

- personal growth to become and be who I am
- relationships and feeling more closely connected to others
- a desire to help the community and make the world a better place.

Internal and external motivation are wired in opposing base value systems. There are many white papers, opinion pieces and studies in this digital age which find that people oriented towards money, status or image report less satisfaction with their lives. They're more depressed and anxious or less vitally energised. Those oriented towards and valuing more quality relationships, self-improvement and community spirit are generally happier and less depressed or anxious. When we get to chapter 5—Relationship value—the single finding from the longest study on human happiness hammers home this point.

That's not to say that external motivation is wrong or bad. In fact, as you'll find in chapter 4—Service value—one's capacity to contribute to the community is drastically increased with greater access to wealth and resources. This is where deeper-seated values and value systems come into play.

Nevertheless, in all aspects of life, external motivation may lose its appeal, punch or shine over time. Take, for example, the 'naughty corner'. Even for a toddler, half an hour eventually becomes easier to handle. After a few short stints, even two hours or multiple nights sent to bed without playtime become a breeze.

There's also another fatal flaw: not everyone is motivated by the same external reward.

A classic simple example to highlight this relates to sales. There's a common misnomer that all salespeople must be driven by money. While many might have it as part of their drive, it ain't necessarily so. Chris, the manager who sparked my thinking deeper into our Value Model, clearly was. One reason I asked him a series of questions was because while I'd been personally successful in sales for many years, even building out bespoke sales capabilities for businesses, the primary motivation wasn't about the money.

Intrinsic motivation decoded

German philosopher, psychologist and author of *Types of Men*, Eduard Spranger (1882–1963) held a view that 'on a lower level, perhaps, the soul is purely biologically determined' yet on a higher level 'the soul participates in objective values which cannot be deduced from the simple value of self-preservation'.

To help appreciate Spranger's concepts, let me first turn to my passion for travel and pose a question: 'Choose a specific city or destination for your next holiday, one you'll truly value. Have you got one?'

Now imagine for a moment how many different responses I'm given when asking that question to hundreds of different people. And what if it were tens or hundreds of thousands of other readers? How many different answers might I get?

A very limited list of answers would be: delving into dining and shopping; multifarious activities in Asian jungles; exploring sights of interest such as the fascinating history and captivating lights of Paris; pursuing a little flop-and-drop solstice; a relaxed respite for a rundown soul via a sand, sea and sun-drenched break in the Bahamas, Maldives or Hawaii; overcoming challenges by climbing mountains; or rugging up for an extraordinary Antarctic rendezvous with seals or penguins.

Yet amid the massive variety, we can begin to group destinations into geographical buckets such as continents, or into desires described by six themes: nature, adventure, museums, shopping, idle leisure and nightlife.

The same is true when we consider intrinsic, internal motivation and drive. This is the essence of Spranger's work, which adds depth of wisdom to how people function via identifiable traits of surface personality types. He defined people's value attitudes as belonging to six primary categories. The 'tour brochure' for these can be summarised as:

1. *theoretical*—dominantly interested in learning and the discovery of truth

2. *economic (utilitarian)*—interested in what is practical and useful

3. *aesthetic*—the highest value being form and harmony (think experiences)

4. *social*—the highest value being love of people and helping others

5. *political*—concerned with power, status or individually getting ahead

6. *traditional*—including religious, value unity and a system for living.

When you observe or ask questions of others you begin to see or hear which underlying intrinsic motivators or value systems are at play.

In the same way that 'Rome', 'Venice', 'Barcelona', 'Tuscany' or even 'the French countryside' and 'the Swiss Alps' are all found in a European catalogue so a desire to 'become an expert', 'be an avid reader of general knowledge' or 'become a scientific theorist' all fall within 'The Theoretical Brochure'.

A primary difference with *how* someone prefers to function, and their intrinsic motivation or *why* is one of fixedness. Someone preferring attention to detail may well dabble with big picture, variety or other preferences, as we've seen. That said, this modus operandi would generally remain a core, stable part of their operating system throughout life. Intrinsic motivation, our drive, has a greater tendency or inclination to periodically shift due to experiences and circumstances.

My own desires as a young leader in his mid twenties travelling Europe were very different from those of the now five-decade-old professional with over 20 years' experience working in my field. When you listen to people's life stories you can hear these deviations in drivers. Using Spranger's model, successful people committed to the bottom line amassing wealth and fortune (economic) or even title (political) may experience a catastrophic illness or a crisis in communication with loved ones and suddenly the value system shifts more towards family or community (social) or enjoying more fully the fruits of life (aesthetic).

Spranger's model, like the others, has continually adapted. His six primary motivators are dissected more deeply as 12 driving forces. Within them lie a mixture of our primary motivators, situational factors and less relevant forces at any moment in time.

Once you learn to discover your truest intrinsic motivators, or those of people you wish to influence or collaborate with, you might consider tailoring rewards and recognition. Adapting any general language, positioning or context of key messages to appeal to individuals' driving force adds value.

Simon Sinek, who sits among the highest viewed TED Talks, in discussing 'how great leaders inspire action' highlights that they start with focusing on the *why.*

Think about it this way. Which goals are the ones you really get excited about? The ones people advise you should be chasing (extrinsic motivators like reward, recognition and punishment, which work fine) or the ones you self-discover and elect (intrinsic motivators like autonomy, mastery and purpose, which set the soul alight)?

Motivation and finding your 'flow'

A final expert to highlight in conversations about desire and drive is one whose work I've appreciated for a long time. Mihaly Csikszentmihalyi is a professor of psychology, sociology and anthropology who creatively dives into realms of happiness and motivation. Csikszentmihalyi is best known as the architect of the notion of 'personal flow'.

Essentially, 'flow' is a focused mental state in which a person performs an activity, the individual being so fully immersed in the process it becomes fulfilling to the point of losing conscious track or awareness of time. With sport we might call this being 'in the zone'. Csikszentmihalyi's 'flow' theory offers a fresh variation by using a graph and labelling the x-axis as 'Challenge' and the y-axis as 'Skills'.

Where the challenge set is very high while the skill set is low, the challenge may create nervousness, frustration and resistance. Performing such a challenge once in a while or over a short period may not be so detrimental, but doing so continually, without improvement to skills, is likely to cause anxiety. It's harder to get into the zone with unhealthy anxiety than optimistic nerves.

Conversely, if the challenge set is very low while the skill set is high, you're more likely to become bored or complacent. Continuing in this manner over a period of time increases the risk of inducing apathy, which is also hardly conducive to being in the zone.

Finding your flow and being in the zone isn't static given skill sets and challenges are always changing. Life isn't inert: we're always learning or facing new challenges. Every time you focus on a new task, your idea of what constitutes a challenge decreases. When a motivated individual finds their 'flow', optimum performance occurs. They kind of forget themselves, they forget their problems and have a sense of doing what it is they are doing. Nothing else matters. It creates a valuable feeling that life is worth living. Flow can happen anywhere: in our personal time, with family, at work or playing sport.

In the same vein that we don't remain in a single state of flow for our entire lives, our overall motivation, or *why*, is just like those aspirational travel destinations.

Sure, you may have a couple of long-standing favourites you have a tendency to visit regularly, but you will explore new territory. And so it is with the second layer of personal value, motivation—your *why*—especially internal motivation, which is a part of you and contributes to your perceptions of value. It also plays out and triggers part of your behaviour, how you may conduct yourself, the actions in what you do.

Speaking of which...

3. Intelligence — IQ & EQ: your ability to *do*

Working for Contiki Holidays was an eye-opener with regard to levels of human intelligence. I recall a colleague of mine who was leading a month-long camping tour in the early 1990s.

They were stunned and more than a little befuddled by one of their passengers. After erecting his allocated tent in Paris on the first night, he asked, in all seriousness, where might his dedicated tent phone plug-in be? After a fairly strange discussion the tourist remained miffed. *What? The mobile accommodation for the duration of the trip, complete with portable tents, doesn't include some kind of portable telephone operating system to plug into each country's network grid?*

Intelligence, as with all aspects of human evolution, dates back to those same hunting, grunting early cave-dwelling ancestors. You can quite imagine that after the discovery of fire, a new short specific sound was added to the tribal vocabulary. A panicked exclamation designed to warn the tribes' cutest little grublets to be careful and not burn their hands or mouths.

We know toddlers have a desire to discover their environment through sensory exploration, touching or tasting everything in sight no matter how sharp, toxic or deadly. This grunt, passed on and translated for centuries, generation to generation, can still be heard with the same level of panic and sweat from parents the world over—the English specific translation being something along the lines of 'Don't touch that! It's dangerous! It's hot!'

Then of course the kid burns their hands or mouth anyway. Which curiously enough highlights a simple yet sizeable clue to intelligence: ultimately, words don't teach anywhere near the manner or depth that experience does.

Early studies decoding intelligence

It's only in moderately recent times—19th century onwards—that we find dedicated, worthy studies to explain this significant phenomenon, namely intelligence, which apparently separates us from many other beasts.

In the early 1900s the French passed a law requiring all children aged 6 to 14 to attend school. As part of due diligence it was decided to elicit insights to help determine which kids may require greater support or assistance in their studies.

Alfred Binet, who invented the first IQ test, tested methodology involving questions and ideas not related to typical school curriculum content and published his research and findings in a paper, 'Experimental Studies of Intelligence', in 1903.

His research included themes like attention span, problem-solving skills, memory and retention. What he found surprising was how some junior children easily answered questions their seniors couldn't—or at least answered them more quickly than the adults.

Medical student Theodore Simon helped Binet further explore and expand the documentation and its findings. In 1905 the Binet–Simon Scale became the first intelligence test, although Binet himself recognised that any 'IQ' test was not valid as a single benchmark for ultimate overall intelligence.

Binet was one of the first to identify the ability of chess-playing masters to navigate and win multiple games, simultaneously, even when playing from memory alone without visible access to the boards.

Binet understood that some people are gifted with a marvellous mind for mnemonic memory yet are still not quite 'intelligent' on what may be deemed a scale of normal.

Another interesting intellectual duo who've played a role in the advanced awareness of intelligence is Lancelot Ware (an Oxford postgraduate student who had administered tests as a researcher during World War II with an interest in a high IQ society for like-minded folks) and Roland Berrill (a rich, aristocratically minded, somewhat booming and colourful, extroverted Australian who had a similar interest in creating an aristocracy of the intellectual). Together, in 1946, they founded the 'high IQ club' Mensa, one of the oldest societies intended as a club for bright minds and brainiacs.

One aspect of Mensa that separates it from other exclusive, top end of town clubs is that membership can't be bought or bribed. Societal status, popularity, celebrity or money can't buy your way in. Membership is only granted to the top 2 per cent of gifted people.

Even then applicants are assessed against a standardised, approved, supervised IQ test. The minimum score is 132, based on the following benchmark ranges for IQ scores:

- 130 plus: extremely high or very superior
- 120–129: very high or superior
- 110–119: high average
- 90–109: average
- 80–89: low average
- 70–79: very low or borderline
- 69 and below: extremely low.

Berrill was apparently disappointed by how many Mensans, the cream of smart people, seemed to come from meagre or humble homes. This highlights another critical consideration about intelligence: any reliance on intellectual smarts alone—the closed or cold-minded manner with which some people act—doesn't equate to solid societal behavioural value.

I think the guy asking about a portable phone exchange to plug into his tent as he travelled around Europe confused Contiki's age bracket of 18 to 35 with his IQ score—as did many others.

The surprising truth about genius

We associate high IQ scores and the label 'genius' with people like Albert Einstein (who never sat an IQ test, but it's estimated his was around 160), yet there are rumblings around a whole bunch of celebrities, too, who fall into this elite top percentile: Nicole

Kidman, Jodie Foster, Arnold Schwarzenegger (and who would dare argue with him!), Natalie Portman, Steve Martin and Conan O'Brien among them. And I knew there was a reason—though I couldn't quite put my finger on why—I've always liked Kate Beckinsale beyond her character in *Underworld*. And Quentin Tarantino: I hear you're in the club too!

'Genius' is one of those words I find ironic too. It's a term often associated with fields of extreme and intellectual—or ground-breaking—advancement in knowledge or creativity. Yet despite its association with scholarly and scientific pursuit, the precise definition—evidence-based, factual, rock-solid proof—of what makes someone undeniably so remains a little elusive.

Applying Albert Einstein's definition of genius—'taking the complex and making it simple'—there's a tonne of people who can do that, yet you wouldn't trust them with a hairdryer close to a shower (or a telephone exchange in a tent).

Alfred Binet correctly hypothesised that there are many factors at play when it comes to social intelligence. Some people with exceptionally high IQs have little to zero common sense or awareness of etiquette and they'll frequently be the most awkward people in the room. Mozart is said to have been one of these people.

Conversely, there are street-smart folk who'd doubtless bomb out badly on any approved, supervised IQ test yet they radiate a light that everyone else will be enticed to swarm to like moths.

This is why 'EQ' (or 'EI') has become popular in more recent years. It was professors Peter Salovey and John Mayer who first coined the label 'emotional intelligence': the ability to be aware of and monitor one's own feelings and emotions in addition to those of others and to adjust one's thinking, choices and actions accordingly.

Salovey and Mayer found that people scoring high on an emotional clarity scale (the aptitude to identify and name a broader range of feelings or emotions) could recover more quickly from upsetting situations.

Additionally, they found people endowed to more accurately read and appraise the emotional state of others were more adept, better equipped and more flexible within social environments, building connections or extending networks.

All of which appeals to common sense and street credibility. Even if you have a deliciously ambiguous IQ score excluding you indefinitely from Mensa membership, you can still improve social intelligence. You can hit the pause button on life, be willing to listen and put a little thought into what's going on for yourself and others. Then reflect before leaping to action and deal with your world through default response, filters and preferences, a standard part of your operating system in *how* you function. EQ means electing a variety of more appropriate responses rather than one-size-fits-all. To improve one's EQ is to improve the quality of all outcomes and relationships.

Daniel Goleman, a psychologist and former science writer for *The New York Times* is frequently associated with emotional intelligence. He's led a prolific dedication researching and writing multiple bestsellers on the subject.

Goleman says 'emotional intelligence begins to develop in the earliest years. All the small exchanges children have with their parents, teachers and with each other carry emotional messages'.

Goleman's work, along with that of other thought leaders, in many ways takes a proverbial sledgehammer to paradigms or prior thinking that IQ alone indicates intelligence or uniquely measures such things as competency, capability, credibility or just plain old ability.

An EQ framework

There are many variations or versions of EQ tools within the marketplace. Common categories for putting emotional intelligence in the spotlight fall under the following.

1. *Self-awareness* — recognising and understanding your emotional range, moods, triggers, auto responses and drives in addition to their impact on others. Someone high on the EQ scale may take a motto that sat above the ancient temples of Delphi to heart: 'Know thyself'.

2. *Self-regulation* — the ability to control and redirect our impulses or moods, including the disruptive ones, appropriately; treating emotions as clues, like signposts, on a road map indicating the best path to take. This includes suspending judgement and leveraging the old adage of 'think before acting' as sound instruction.

3. *Motivation/drive* — in the context of EQ, drive extends beyond intrinsic motivators such as knowledge and truth and relates to tenacity. It taps into passion or propensity to continue the pursuit of goals with persistence.

4. *Social awareness* — suspending all judgement and seeking to recognise and understand the emotional states and makeup of others. It's having awareness that everything you say or do has the power to impact, for better or worse, everyone around you.

5. *Social regulation/skills* — as the external culmination of EQ in action, this relates to the way we communicate with and treat others. It's having an ability to influence and offer perspective around the emotional clarity of others, and proficiently taking ownership of managing all relationships and networks.

Looking at EQ through the filters of this framework there are patterns that emerge. Upon reflection you may even identify which may be your strengths, or conversely areas of opportunity to work on:

- *intrapersonal pattern (self)—*
  self-awareness + self-regulation

  vs

- *interpersonal pattern (others)—*
  social awareness + social regulation

  and

- *knowledge awareness pattern—*
  self-awareness + social awareness

  vs

- *regulation and action pattern—*
  self-regulation + social regulation.

How our emotions play out

Our emotional states and moods, checked or unchecked, positive or negative, play a vital role in our conscious response choices, as opposed to auto reactions. They also have an impact on our own health and wellbeing as well as the quality of relationships in all aspects of our world.

Negative emotional states tend to increase blood pressure and heart rate; create muscle tension and increase adrenaline and cortisol (a stress hormone); make our pupils dilate; and trigger cold, sweaty palms. In other words, the same hardwiring associated with a typical fight-or-flight response, even when not warranted.

Positive emotional states have a tendency to improve immune function; decrease heart rate or blood pressure; improve clarity in decision-making, concentration or focus; relax the body;

and ultimately allow us to be in a response state of thoughtful conscious choice rather than reaction:

1. we have ideas or thoughts about situations or things in our life

2. regardless of whether they are good or bad, these thoughts generate feelings (emotional states)

3. our feelings and emotional states determine and drive our actions

4. the actions we take create a reaction and deliver our results

5. the results may create a new belief or reinforce an existing one.

And so our emotional states and moods have the power to perpetuate cycles of behaviour and perceptions of value.

Inspirational speaker and author Esther (Abraham) Hicks would say 'a belief is an idea reinforced with emotion and feeling that you've held onto for a long time'. This is why a simple idea to improve overall EQ may be finding—authentically—things, people and situations that make you feel good. Take your attention away from the energy-sucking black holes.

We all experience a vast range of feelings on a daily basis. Some can describe them in more detail than others. As Hermione Granger said to Ron Weasley in *Harry Potter and the Order of the Phoenix*, 'Just because you've got the emotional range of a teaspoon doesn't mean we all have!'

Negative emotions needn't necessarily be a bad thing. As the Dalai Lama points out, feelings are not destructive in themselves: they only become destructive when their intensity is out of proportion to the situation or when they arise in situations that do not warrant them.

Think about it this way. You can be angry without acting out the anger. In fact there's potentially nothing more intimidating than someone in full control of their emotions very calmly stating, 'You have no idea. How angry I am. Right now'.

It tends to demand attention and respect way more than pots and pans flying across a room or fists flying through the air. Emotional expression directed as physical violence is merely one among a plethora of destructive intensities that are all too frequently way out of proportion when applied to situations.

Blending layers of behaviour

Earlier in the chapter I referenced that the behavioural layer of *how* we function has a tendency to remain a preferred consistent throughout life. Our preferences may lend themselves to specific skills or traits.

We discussed that our *why* or intrinsic motivation changes according to circumstances, evolving personal growth or different stages of life.

EQ has similarity with both. Some preferences on how to function, or indeed intrinsic drivers, may naturally lend themselves to different aspects of EQ. Emotional intelligence is a skill that doesn't remain static. It can advance or regress.

You can always keep improving through practical strategies consistently put into action. Where the energy goes, the traction flows.

Our early ancestors showed signs of EQ: creating social bonds that led to the formation of small tribes who hunted collaboratively in packs, huddled together for warmth, and cared for the ill and elders. All of which was managed without traditional intelligence associated with IQ or even the sophistication of a common spoken tongue.

Our overall intelligence (or perception of value) isn't exactly something we're critically born with. Like other animals, we may be super cute in infancy but we're really quite useless. Newborn elephants are among the most advanced. They're coerced so that they learn to stand within minutes of birth. They have to, otherwise they'd perish from not being able to drink their mother's milk. Baby dolphins are born with complex echolocation biosonar, which they rapidly begin experimenting with and expanding within days. We, on the other hand, lie for months in a cot, unable to do anything other than piss, fart, poo, burp, spit, drool and puke—often simultaneously. I tell you what, it's a damn good job we are super cute or our parents might be tempted to trade us in rather than nurturing and infusing us with value and love over long periods of time.

Even once we're old enough to run around generally making a nuisance of ourselves, like baby elephants (who really are very cute), we're still rather daft. Other animals learn quickly to fend for themselves without quite so many f*ck ups.

You won't hear a mummy elephant trumpeting the equivalent of our ancestors' grunts: 'Don't touch that! It's hot!'

Intelligence, especially the emotional kind, is something you can improve and develop over time. And it's worth it.

The dark side of intelligence

So, naturally, while on the topic of emotional intelligence, let's talk about psychopaths.

There are a few people among the general populous falling outside the spectrum of 'normal'. In other words, somewhat incapacitated to develop their EQ potential.

Psychopaths and sociopaths have a complete disregard for the safety, rights or concern of others.

Manipulation, deceit or deliberate cunning are a part of their chosen personal weapons of choice. They don't have the capacity to feel remorse or guilt the way others do.

Researchers debate, controversially at times, different aspects of both of these subsets. There are those working in the field who'd somewhat argue a case of genetic predisposition, a warrior gene that may be present in the case of psychopaths. Even then the environment—a lack of nurturing—unleashes the sleeping devil that hides inside.

Sociopaths, on the other hand, are more frequently considered a creation of their environments. Either a lack of nurturing or extremities in life experiences twist a pure-born cherub into a demon. You can't see a sociopath in the rather useless but cute, wee bundle of joy in the cot.

Psychopaths manage to hide and blend into society due to an ability to create a table of responses. That capacity, as evil as it is, shows signs of intelligence. They may not feel any emotion, yet they recognise something in how others react so they recreate or mimic it.

Narcissists differ in that it's all about them. No, really. It is. Sociopaths and psychopaths may ask cunning questions or introduce topics of importance to you, to build an artificial trust. Making it about you may be a part of their path to power. Narcissists, on the other hand, introduce topics of interest about them. Passive-aggressive behaviours, such as silent treatment or severance, fall among the preferred weapons of choice in their vicious armoury of vanity. All are used to perpetuate a primary purpose fuelling admiration of their own self-worth and value, often at the expense of others.

Studies have been shared suggesting a potentially higher ratio of psychopaths in senior C-suite roles than in other areas of the workplace. It was industrial psychologist Paul Babiak and criminal psychologist Robert D Hare who described this phenomenon of workplace psychopaths as 'snakes in suits', estimating that around 1 per cent of the general population (that's a freaking lot!) meets the clinical criteria for psychopathy.

CEOs aren't alone in being tarred with the undesirable brush: lawyers, media personalities, sales people, police officers, clergy, journalists, surgeons and chefs all fall—according to the conclusions of Kevin Dutton, a British psychologist, in his

'Great British Psychopath Survey'—among professions with the highest proportional rates. When you see Gordon Ramsay flying off the handle this may just have some merit.

There has been an escalation of people dishing out labels of psychos, sociopaths or narcissists within their circle. The reality is that while the law of probability suggests we may well cross paths with individuals who would tick boxes for credible clinically diagnosed versions of each, we'd usually do so unknowingly. More commonly these slurs and slanders are a case of mistaken identity. We observe people demonstrating behaviours born from lower skills in specific facets of EQ—you know, crassly singing aloud songs telling anyone who doesn't love them to kiss their arse! Like Mozart is documented as doing! And it takes high EQ to suspend judgement.

Not everyone who dishes out silent treatment is a narcissist. Social awkwardness or a lack of empathy are frequently tied to prior experiences that perhaps you're not aware of. Not everyone who shows an obvious disregard in valuing others is a psycho, sociopath or narcissist. They may be operating from a space of ego further magnified by a lack of EQ...I don't know why...I can't imagine...but for some strange reason a picture of Donald Trump springs to mind.

Regardless, developing a higher EQ means continually working on yourself, simultaneously concerning yourself less in the judgement of others. Treat people as you wish to be treated. Well, unless of course you're a psychopath, in which case, for the record, I'm not suggesting for a moment you slice, dice and dish others around you, Hannibal Lecter style, with fava beans and a nice Chianti.

Reflect on your world. Untangle the automatic emotional responses you may have learned along the way to date. Redirect disruptive impulses. Continue with persistence towards goals that excite and drive you, doing so with empathy and consideration of the goals and rights of others. Learn to adapt your communication and capacity to influence along the way.

How others behave has nothing to do with you. Having a high EQ means realising no-one, other than you, has power over you. No matter how it seems.

If you do relinquish this power by saying to someone 'you make me feel [insert emotional buzz word here], then ask them to kindly flip the switch to prevent your inner negativity. That's likely going to sound rather daft because deep down you know you can't. There is no switch. If you feel a certain way it's because on some level you're choosing it.

Epictetus was a 1st century slave who navigated a life path to becoming a philosopher. You've likely heard variations of one of his views: 'It's not what happens to you, but how you react to it that matters'.

To remain cool, not allowing external situations to impact your own equilibrium, simultaneously being stalwart in consideration of others is indicative of a higher EQ.

Even then, the kindest, most highly evolved, loving people on the planet aren't adored by everyone. Life doesn't automatically become a bed of roses. I'll say it again: *It's never what happens that's important. It's how you choose to respond.* You always have a choice of responses, even when things feel unfair or hopeless. Behavioural scientist, author and motivational speaker Steve Maraboli states that 'you express the truth of your character with the choice of your actions'. In other words, what you do says a lot about your character and values.

Which leads us nicely to the final layer of the Value Model's personal value chapter. Because what you choose to do has a whole lot to do with *who* you really are.

4. Everything else: *who* am I?

Words don't teach, life experience does. Words may hold power to gain a fresh perspective, but participation—living life—imparts influences as the greatest educator. People sometimes need to fall on their own sword in order to learn. Failing isn't negative. The contrast in life, including harsh, unpleasant circumstances, unlocks the best learnings. Like everyone, I've faced my own challenges. Many date back to childhood.

My parents tell me I was a happy and quiet child. I could be left to my own devices where I'd joyfully play with my toys or wonder at the world without fuss. That solitary silence has followed me like a shadow in the five decades since, a theme relevant both here and later when we drill into the perception of relationship value.

When I was little we moved homes a lot. My father, a naval veteran for 20-plus years, was frequently transferred base-to-base or away at sea for months at a time. When I was aged four we planted firm roots in Scotland.

I vaguely recall living in Edinburgh before moving to South Queensferry on the Firth of Forth. It was a shorter trip for Dad to Rosyth dockyard over the Forth Bridge in Fyfe.

Being born in England yet raised in Scotland opens strange mindset doors. I recall being politely labelled a 'Sassenach' and laughed at for anything. More impolitely, all too frequently, the haranguing was far worse. You know, I was the English c***, f*cker and the likes.

It's confusing to grasp why a nativity location or origin of descendancy were such catastrophic birth defects. Being born English, raised in Scotland, with some Scottish heritage on my grandma's side of the family, became an early catalyst for bullying. Perhaps the additional silent ostracism and self-loathing that was to come were somewhat inevitable. You just don't know that when you're four.

I do recall having the hell kicked out of me on most days in the littlies playground starting from primary school level one. Some days I was lucky enough to be of value during every play break as a practice punch bag. Four and five year olds may not pack a hook like Mike Tyson, yet to another rug rat, slight in build, every whack did damage. And we're not just talking physically. The wallopings did fall in regularity with each passing primary school year. I do believe though it's one reason I became so good at athletics—one of the fastest kids. I was like Forrest Gump: for the longest time, I don't know why I didn't hit back, I'd just run. Except for this one time years later, primary school Year 6 or 7, when I was aged around 10. Finding myself cornered against a schoolyard wall, for some reason the frustration and fury channelled down my arm to a curled fist instead of my legs to winged feet. I walloped the main antagonist a mighty, unexpected, uppercut and side blow. It wasn't canvas flooring but it was enough to stun and shock, creating an easier escape. The bizarre thing is that later that night my mum received a phone call from the mother of the boy in question asking that I leave Murray alone!

Physical assault was only the surface. Verbal harassment, exclusion or silent treatment over the years was equally hurtful, in fact more so, than being bashed up. Bruises and cuts disappear and heal. Ostracism creates hidden scars not so easily mended or reconciled.

Kids seem to learn early that juvenile powerplays work better than smacking someone about. Silent treatment and mind manipulation (including gaslighting) inflict pain without the annoyance of being caught by the evidence of visible marks of a tangible assault. That's why clinical narcissists also use these mean mechanisms as preferred weapons from their armoury. These passive-aggressive behaviours may seem innocent to the rest of the world, a disguise of taking the high ground, where the reality is anything but.

Kids may know no better. Especially if they've been role-modelled such behaviour.

Adults, without an actual clinical diagnosis of narcissism may have prejudices, a different value system, their own deep-seated personal devils, fears, limiting beliefs or patterns from prior experiences to draw upon. They may also be simply operating from lower ranges of emotional intelligence. It's why with the work I now do there are occasions when I share some insight.

Research suggests the simple act of ostracism may activate the same neural pathways and areas of the brain associated with physical pain. Think about that for a moment: to deliberately cold shoulder another soul is no better than physical assault. The same is true for malicious gossip, rumour or lies. Once you know that sound bite of information you can't pretend anymore not to know it, which creates an opportunity to work on your emotional intelligence. You get to show the world the true nature of your character anew every day. The value we bring is demonstrated by the choice of our actions, not the emptiness (or deliberate silence) of words alone.

I share the first part of this personal childhood story because it powerfully highlights two destructive layers (debilitating demons that cause a breakdown in self-confidence, self-worth and perception of value):

1. *Life experiences—external behaviour and situations:*

   - being told you're no good or being mistreated by others (physically, verbally or mentally)

   - being pre-conditioned by environments to specific mindsets and responses.

2. *Life experiences—internal dialogue translated to behaviour:*

   - negative self-talk or putting ourselves down

   - selecting our preferred choice of responses, including barriers/walls we build

   - learning habitual protective mechanisms (aloof, cold, distant, judging), which may serve as a defence in childhood but no longer serve us as adults.

These scenarios in my childhood all played havoc with my self-confidence and self-worth and impacted me for quite a period of time. This included a stage over many months, I forget at what age, where I stopped eating properly. I adopted a really bad habit of disposing of my lunches by donation to the class gannets or tossing the food away.

There were times I'd forgotten to do either so to discard the evidence I'd find ingenious ways (or so I thought) of stuffing foil-wrapped grub in various cupboards, nooks and crannies at home. This plan, born in the confused brain of a child, was hardly mastermind. The decaying, rotten food was easily sniffed out by parental instincts. Wedging squashed foil packages among clothes or under the bed and mattress is like trying to hide a dead body in plain sight really, and no doubt smells just as bad. There was also the physical evidence. Gradually withering down to ribs and bone, I looked like a skinny, sickly child for quite some time.

When my mother figured out what was happening she strategised corrective measures enforcing a 'go home for lunch' rule or, on the days she was working part time, a visit to the village bakery where she could keep an eye on me. Both ensured eating patterns were improved, but they were a bloody long hike and, to some degree, impacted social blending, which was already a little stretched. So now there were two more reasons I deserved a hiding:

'Skinny and a Sassenach! Screw you!' (Wallop!)

'Hey no friends! F*ck off!' (Smack!)

On a different occasion a couple of years on, I was playing marbles with my eldest brother on the side of the road. I had one of those rectangular leather back satchels. Mine seemed to protrude beyond my shoulder blades further than most, possibly due to my slight frame. A passing school bus clipped it and sent me flying. I was knocked unconscious for a few minutes. I do remember waking up to a rotund, sweaty, worried-looking driver shaking me saying, 'Are you okay son, are you okay?' His passengers had a different opinion. It was the Catholic kids' school bus.

'Haha! F*cking got one! Screw you ya skinny Sassenach, proddy bastard!'

The driver, climbing back in his vehicle somewhat relieved, had accidentally delivered the hiding that usually followed such abuse. I was bewildered, with a lump almost the size of a golf ball already visible on my head. Plus I was puzzled, as I wasn't actively practising any religion. I watched as the bus drew away, the entire overcrowded back row celebrating and dishing out two fingers in contempt, disappointed I was still breathing. Ah well. At least my eating habits had improved by this stage.

My work now includes aspects of human behaviour and development so it's easy to identify early self-destructive, devaluing behaviours. Some I kept longer than need be. Others, at times, still attempt to rear their heads. If we're not careful or conscious, these scars and behaviours (to ourselves or others) creep in, like saboteurs, as habitual choices into adulthood.

We reach for fight-or-flight responses even when the situation doesn't warrant it or long after it serves any purpose. For me running away as a child felt like the best defensive option. As a mature adult, better equipped mentally and physically, making assumptions or living in avoidance, even of conversations, isn't a great resolve.

Everyone carries their own experiences

I recall an incident from one of those Contiki hotel tours. The first day was always a little chaotic with so many logistic and organisational responsibilities, one of which was confirming final room requirements for the entire trip. Before we left London, approximate room numbers had been put on hold, but we might have last minute changes to consider. These were the days of more manual labour checks, less automation you understand.

Given our first hotel for that very night was one of the many tasks to complete en route, I was double checking names and ensuring people had been paired together appropriately. Any friends booked and travelling together would expect to be roomed together too. If you had any couples, you'd take note and try your best to get double rooms rather than twin ones. Some people, paying a slightly higher premium, elected the privacy of a single room so you'd want to make sure they got it. Plus, more common were people electing to pay a standard price for a twin room although travelling alone or even selecting a slightly more budget friendly triple room rate.

So a part of checking the final list was making sure that single travellers who'd elected a twin room had been matched with another single person, same gender, with the same nomination.

After finalising my list I was armed to phone the hotel in Amsterdam from our final pit stop a couple of hours prior to arrival. As I confirmed the requirements they told me the relevant room numbers for different room types over the phone and I quickly scribbled them down. After this, the process was easier as I could confirm the list for the whole tour. Just this first day was a little more manic.

Departing the service stop on this last leg I then got on the microphone to share, by surnames, the room numbers for this first hotel. As I completed sharing this I could see one female passenger leave the back seat to make her way to the front. I'd toured long enough to know something had happened to annoy her. I just couldn't easily figure out what.

In the time it took for her to walk the length of the coach my mind deduced it had to be something in the rooming list. Glancing through, I noticed only one peculiarity that may be involved but couldn't deduce what the problem was. I suspected, correctly as it were. This passenger turned out to be one of two ladies paired in a twin room. As she sat down on the front step next to my seat I smiled and asked if I could help. Her response completely caught me off guard. It was nowhere in the vicinity of anything my mind was churning in solution thinking:

'So Mark, I just want to know if you're an out and out racist or selectively so?'

Wow! So get this. It turns out this passenger, from New York, a single female travelling alone had nominated sharing a twin room. The computer system had paired her with another single female travelling alone electing twin share, randomly also from the United States. Their names on the computer-generated, non-alphabetical rooming list happened to be the last twin room detailed on the draft. Therefore I'd written the last number from that hasty phone call against their names printed on the draft. Every room was on level 2 except theirs, which was on level 7. The final coincidence, the one to ignite her fuse, both single females were black.

My first response was to pause. And then to say I was sorry. Sorry for whatever experiences she'd endured in a lifetime to assume, within a fraction of a second, the room allocation was a deliberate act of racism on my part.

I then transparently explained the entire process. Within minutes she was happy and cool. We got on well and it turned out to be an awesome tour. This experience, one of many on those Contiki tours, reaffirms how quickly we can leap to judgement or belief patterns based on prior experiences. When it ain't always necessarily so.

I'm far happier this passenger took the time to transparently have the conversation straight away to figure it out. There are plenty of others who silently accept the niggling inner voice.

As a middle-aged, white male, I do understand and accept my life has been far cushier than others, yet this privilege everybody speaks of isn't exactly the case either. I was ostracised based on race for the pale white skin of an Englishman rather than the pale blue of a Scot.

I don't believe for a moment I've had it tough (childhood or life) in comparison to others. But the demons we each face that impact our perception of self-worth and value are not about comparison. One person's detrimental battles may still debilitate their ability to value themselves or add value to others in their world.

Jack Canfield, a co-author of *Chicken Soup for the Soul*, says in a documentary titled *The Secret*, that everybody has stuff going on and that's just called 'so what!' and that a far better internal dialogue to have is 'so what are you going to do about it?'

Learn to suspend judgement. You'll never know the experiences another person has endured that become a part of their behavioural makeup and actions.

On the flip side, if you ever find yourself on the receiving end of definite anti-social behaviours (bullying, prejudice or pretty awful treatment dressed up dozens of ways) remind yourself that it's not actually about you (unless of course you've behaved poorly in the first place by acting nasty, toxic or hurtful).

Fight-or-flight 'meaning-making machines'

Environment and conditioning influence who we become. Some people live in countries or communities where long-standing traditions and expectations inhibit their basic right to be who they really are. Others have been fed prejudicial ideologies as a toddler. Those uncontested beliefs from formative years, like parents or generations before, may fester and become a part of who they are. Unless, of course, they consciously elect to be open minded and exploratory. Some people have limiting beliefs, assumptions and even fears that hold them back for years. They are 'meaning-making machines', anchoring definition to experiences. The situation acts like the tiny piece of grit, an annoying irritant that an oyster might coat with layer upon layer of nacre to protect itself.

In this case the wisdom we anchor as definitive, creating blueprints for thoughts or future patterns of behaviour, may not be quite so precious as mother of pearl.

Human beings are hardwired with some common natural limiting beliefs or fears such as:

- fear of dying
- fear of social rejection or abandonment
- fear of humiliation
- fear of losing control.

While many of us share the commonality of some of these fears, the vast majority we hoard are born from experiences of our own lives.

Fears and limiting beliefs are not necessarily always a bad thing. They serve to protect us from making a dangerous or reckless decision and are a key reason for the survival of our species. This 'fight-or-flight' hardwiring has proven to be a great device in the armoury of human tools. The problem is that our fight-or-flight mechanism these days kicks in for scenarios or situations that are not as dangerous as our amygdala may suggest.

A difficult looming conversation with the boss is not a battle for survival with a sabre-toothed tiger. Dealing with issues in our relationships is not as dangerous as being pushed out of a tribe into the wilds of the savannah to fend for ourselves.

These fight-or-flight responses may also become a core part of who we are. They are why, when you get intimate with someone, the idea of vulnerability can create the urge to run, or when crammed into a crowd heading through a darkened tunnel you have this almost uncontrollable urge to scream.

Among 'the everything else of life' there are hundreds of labels for emotions but laid out on a see-saw they are weighted on either side by the two most powerful emotions: love and fear.

As Elisabeth Kübler-Ross, a Swiss-American psychiatrist said, 'All positive emotions come from love, all negative emotions from fear'.

Love or fear?

That is the decision that defines you. When your fears, learned from prior experiences, are restricting your world, perhaps it's time to tackle them head on.

Fear is blame based. Love is accepting.

Fear drives a desire to control. Love allows freedom and detachment.

Fear kills passion. Love enlivens and ignites it.

Fear is the saboteur that prevents you from making positive changes.

Love is the superhero that makes everything possible.

Love is the energy that expands. Fear is the energy that contracts.

Every life event is an opportunity to choose love over fear.

Work with all the layers of everything else, the life experiences that have partially sculpted and forged you. Listen to your heart and mind. Challenge outdated, debilitating ideas. Work through your fears—don't be defined by them—doing so is where your self-worth and value, as with love, expands all possibilities.

Personal value
Tools, tips and self-reflEQtion

We can blend the four layers of personal value together in the manner of a thick onion soup:

1. Preferences in behaviour: *how* we function.

2. Motivation or drive for behaviour: our *why* at any moment in time.

3. Competence or intelligence to adapt and *do*: filters like IQ and EQ.

4. Other factors influencing *who* we are: life experience and everything else.

These layers bubble and simmer together, compounding or softening different ingredients or specific traits. They also influence our value: who we really are at the core of it all. To highlight this I'll quickly share two historical characters, side by side as:

- similar preference in style: dominant and influential types

- similar motivations: individualistic politicians driven to succeed

- similarity in skills and intelligence: cunning orators who could influence
- some similarity in life experiences: not always plain sailing and included war.

Yet their underlying values and value systems—vastly different—determined their overall legacy judged by history in polarising ways. Who are they?

Winston Churchill and Adolf Hitler.

Learning is lifelong. Challenge life's lessons to unlearn, relearn and continually learn so the patterns of behaviour fuelling our choices are relevant and improve the quality of value we add to all aspects of our world.

Personal value is the equivalent of the fifth divine element, the one known as aether. It's a culmination of all our experiences, opinions, preferences, biases, prejudices and values. The other four values in the Value Model (tangible, emotional, service and relationship) are like the four classical elements. What we find is that components within each will resonate more than others because of who we are and how we function.

As for polishing up on personally adding value, there are already many clues in the descriptions and stories shared in this chapter. Here are some additional prompts to consider. (You can access more in my online supporting content.)

Preference and type adoption

Identify *how* you really like to function: embrace your strengths. Manage the areas you are less attracted to doing. It's okay. Nobody is great at everything.

Preference and type adaptation

Think about others around you. Make an effort to identify how they prefer to function. Be the first to adapt your manner of approach, methods of communication and use a more conscious choice of language and words. You don't need to change who you are to improve the quality of all relationships.

Motivation: What's your why?

Do you know what's driving you? Tap into the *why* of your inner drive, then align your goals, self-rewards and choices.

Motivation: The why of others

Ask questions to figure out what's driving those around you. What are their goals and motivations? Don't assume they are the same as yours. You can then adapt your approach, collaboration and communication.

Work on improving your intelligence: EQ

Read through the five categories in the EQ framework again. Ask questions and set simple actions around the ones you know you wish to improve on.

Regular planning for skills, competence and attitude

Set time aside each month for the business of continual learning. Which skills should you study? All of them: soft, hard, specialist. You should never be so busy that you sacrifice learning. The world keeps changing and to stop learning is assuredly to get left behind.

Let go of past or limiting beliefs

What assumptions, patterns of behaviour, fears or limitations have you been holding onto? Do any spring to mind that may be restricting value in your life: social circles, career and relationships? If so, identify an action plan to challenge, update or leave them behind.

What are your values?

You will have some. What are they? What are the things that are most important to you: the manner in which you live, play and work? Can you define what's really important? Making choices aligned with these values will contribute to your happiness and fulfillment. They will make prioritisation and decision making easier.

2

Tangible value

The value language of business

Writer and philosopher Ayn Rand wrote, 'Money is only a tool. It will take you wherever you wish, but it will not replace you as the driver'.

Chris, the manager I asked the question to initially, like us all, gave clues to the total combination of his own personal value in the way he leaped to define value. As a results-driven, dominant individual motivated by utility, he had an eagle-eyed focus on bottom-line returns. His answer of 'what someone is willing to pay' is hardly surprising. Most people with a strong inclination towards tangible value give similar responses when prompted, for example:

- 'You get back more than you put in.'
- 'The cost minus the benefit leaves you the value.'
- 'You can measure the results.'
- 'It's worth what it costs.'

The definition of tangible is 'perceptible to touch'. In the business world, tangible value means that something is measurable.

Business tangibility is shifting. In Australia you can register a company name in less than 15 minutes for a fee of a little over $500 (including GST). Yet the corporation exists in name alone: there are no premises, employees or even products to speak of—nothing tangible. Even with continued growth, the business may continue offering invisible products serviced by automation and algorithms with little human touch, from premises containing no doors or windows to speak of (unless your mobile office is a PC and not a Macintosh!).

All business owners know and deal with tangible value on a quarterly or annual basis with forms such as a **Business Activity Statement**, where:

1A (GST on sales) – 1B (GST on purchases) = $ amount owed to / due from the ATO

John Anderson, founder of Contiki Holidays, shares a wonderful story from the early days. An oversight in budgeting meant he foresaw an inability to complete an itinerary as planned. He calculated how much it would cost to get all passengers back to London. He put that amount safely aside. He gambled the remainder on Monte Carlo tables. Fortune favoured his boldness, an epic decision that I, like hundreds of thousands of others, appreciated.

I'm no economist, maths genius or detailed analyst. I'm not drawn to data patterns or dollar returns the way some people are. That said, I do appreciate the importance of tangible value. As with mathematicians, physicists, economists and many a scientist, I too find analysis captured in quantitative and qualitative data important, and as we'll find out, quite beautiful.

In a product or service exchange the item itself is the tangible value. But the primary perceptions determining tangible value are ones you can't really touch. This is one thing we can all relate to. Success, since the earliest days of corporations some 200 years ago, has been perceived in metrics.

Leaders on the right side of the law may smile or cry, rejoice or bemoan, massage or strategise these indicators with a goal of continually improving the bottom line. Others, drawn to the dark side of corruption, may edit, spin or fall into deceit if twisting the quantifiable data improves appeal to the perception of others.

All metrics in business are really only the lagging indicators of other more important measures: a total sum of personal value actions, behaviours or even collective culture.

Regardless whether professionally or personally, we all have benchmarks, reports and measures in our lives that we budget, debate, deliberate, drool over, stress about or even celebrate. These measures of evidence, business and pleasure are the four metrics we benchmark to prove or feel the worth of tangible value.

Tangible value in a nutshell

The four metrics of tangible value are the benchmarks we use daily in business:

1. A history of money
2. Percentages
3. Numbers
4. Time.

1. A history of money

Where do all the dollars come from? Or, in the style of Jerry Maguire hollering down a phone line at the top of his lungs, 'Show me the money!' Let's dissect and answer that question in terms of tangible value.

Sources like Investopedia are gold for quick insights. And take a peek at the Netflix release of Steven Soderbergh's movie *The Laundromat*. The comedic drama unravels money laundering, questionable practices and the collapse of shell companies. It also has some of the best one-liners: 'Credit is an invention that meant you no longer needed to carry around…millions of bananas on slips of paper…Credit said that even if you didn't have all the bananas you need…you could borrow bananas from the future'.

But let's not get ahead of ourselves. In the beginning, there were no dollars (or other currencies as such). Trade and wealth were created and represented by the exchange of goods and services. This resourceful notion is known as the bartering system. You know, swapsies!

The hunter-gatherers might have offered some sharpened stones or tasty wee trimmings of meat in return for a lovely bespoke fur—and some juicy berries on the side for extra value. Leaders or elders may have had special privileges yet tribes still strived to amass communal wealth collaboratively with a common goal: continuance and survival. The tools or weapons you'd give in exchange could be considered an early wage for hands-on services rendered to help fall a mammoth.

While leading Contiki tours, I discovered exciting barter systems still thriving. For example I know for a fact at one time you could trade really ugly or outdated staff uniforms—you know, the bright peacock tour rep clothes—so as not to be missed by lost passengers. In return for these luminous accoutrements you'd procure dodgy, black-market CDs with strange titles: a result of strained Russian hearing phonetically, inaccurately translating lyrics meant the Phil Collins classic 'I Wish It Would Rain Down' became 'I Wish If Would Rain Sewn'. Depending on how ugly or stupendous the shirt was, the going rate fell somewhere between two and four CDs. Peers would ask ahead of time if you were going and load you up with their unwanted shirts. I have no idea why but for some obscure reason on the outskirts of Tver, on the road to Moscow, in the 1990s, pass-me-down Contiki clothing held the same demand as the most outrageous offerings from any Versace Baroque range.

Through various historical periods different items became elevated in status. Some were obvious for immediate survival — others less so. Roman soldiers at one point earned salt for their service. The expensive commodity was used to extend the life of food. Hence it was a part of their 'salary'.

As communities grew and trade circles broadened this typical model of exchange became a little trickier to manage. It's fine when you're Rupert the rope maker delivering lengths of string to Henry the hay-bale guy who lives just a few huts up. But what about Bill the baker? A trip to his village 25 kilometres away becomes a logistical nightmare. Imagine having to lug stacks of bound hay bales or weighted weapons in order to, literally, get your daily bread.

Even today, travelling for trade still exists. We've all seen pictorial evidence from developing countries. There's Fred the fake T-shirt dude with his amazingly sturdy pedal pushbike. The 200 bags of knock-off T-shirts are stacked precariously, ready to topple. Often you'll find the faithful co-worker perched dangerously on the handlebars trying to steady it all. It's a testament to the human spirit that we'll always find a way of survival, earning our daily bread with whatever worn-out tools may be at hand.

From trade to tokens to coins

In the evolution of money though, it became clear that breaking your back wasn't sustainable. Far easier was to have traded goods or services represented by tokens. Sometimes these were engraved with specific symbols portraying the item in question. Other times those standard tokens became agreed amounts or weights personifying the value of the items in question.

But commodities weren't and aren't always equal in value. An example being that a weapon was always worth multiple times the token required for a loaf of bread. Historically speaking, delivering death took priority over food delivery. You'd have to do one in order to procure a logistical supply chain for the other. Not much has changed in some ways in that regard. Governments and people can be screwy.

I remember stumbling across old tales in my 10 years working for Contiki in Europe: stories suggesting even beer was considered a token for tender. Some criminals convicted of capital crimes would forfeit or be forced to make liquid amber payment by the barrel to victims' families as a form of compensation. (This was in addition to harsh sentencing, which might have included the cost of their life, of course.) Perhaps that's where the expression 'I could murder for a beer' comes from.

It's amazing what might constitute a token. Anything could be used really, so long as it was mutually recognised: whales' teeth, feathers or smooth stones are all documented among the earliest forms of 'dough', our daily bread also becoming a moniker for money.

Amassing tokens became associated with wealth and power. Kings and leaders began minting their own. These 'coins' became intrinsically linked to monetary tangible value in their own right due to the nature of the materials used: silver and gold.

Paper money coincided with the invention of block printing, circa 1200 CE. The Chinese figured they could keep real coins safe from theft under lock and key in vaults at the palace. It's said that Marco Polo brought the idea of paper money back with him to Italy. (Is there anything Marco Polo didn't secure from his travels to the Far East?) So coins and paper money began to co-exist.

In the 1600s, paper money became standard in European banking systems with the British pound dominating. Governance created the standard lines of text that 'promised to pay the bearer on demand' the appropriate sum indicated. Paper was far easier to carry than weighted bags of coins, even if, by this time, some coins had been replaced by cheaper, lighter base metals worth intrinsically far less than the face value of the coin itself.

The power and rule of European currency, in particular British pounds, were to be toppled from their number one spot. Colonists in the New World were forced to pay excessive taxes while simultaneously being disadvantaged in access to British pounds. They rebelled in 1773 in the form of the infamous Boston Tea Party, which was the catalyst for a patriotic uprising. The loss of potential territory amid an ever-expanding empire was a princely sum indeed to the bloated, stingy Brits. But American independence (1776) was a catalyst that ultimately cost the British far more—the balance of monetary power—and the US economy and currency (the dollar) became a main player.

The 'gold standard' was born as a system to protect value. Any wad of paper constituting currency was directly linked to a fixed amount in gold, thus further reducing risk or exposure through mechanisms of counterfeit or fraud.

Economic collapse and depression

Economies around the world have crashed on multiple occasions during historical periods of political upheaval, civil unrest, poor policymaking or hyperinflation. Post-World War I was a prime example. Germany was held accountable as the primary instigator. Therefore the terms laid out in the Treaty of Versailles slapped them with hefty cash penalties in addition to fines of vital industrial lands or means of production.

Germany suspended its version of the gold standard, assuring convertibility from currency to gold. Enter a series of other poor economic choices and before you knew it, you might find yourself roving around Berlin sweating profusely in your Lederhosen, pushing a wheelbarrow full of money.

In the United States, while the Federal Reserve currency of 'greenbacks' (so named because one side of the standard foldable money was dyed with green ink) was backed and assured by the government for payment of public or private debts, it wasn't allowed to be exchanged for the tangible value it represented in silver or gold. And herein lies a trend-setting pattern that still has worldwide impact to this day: the idea that sheer optimism, confidence or faith in countries' economies plays a significant factor in the perceived value of any currency.

Systems evolved where bankers came to realise depositors didn't tend to ask for their money all at once. So, on paper at least, they always had excess dollars to play with, which allowed them to win by amassing wealth in two new ways. First, obviously, they paid less interest as a bonus on any money deposited. They would then take the money, which wasn't theirs, lend it out and charge a higher rate of interest. Had anyone other than banks or governments thought to have done this it would have been criminal. Second, a wizard of an idea: why not lend money we don't even have? It's not like the idea of securities or gold standard mattered as much anymore. And people aren't all clambering to access it so who's to ever know about this alchemy!

It all seemed a pretty cool idea until the stock market crash in 1929. Amid all the uncertainty, anxious investors, worried about the security of their hard-earned cash, triggered a run on the banks.

More than 600 banks failed and totally collapsed—including New York's Bank of the United States to the tune of over $200 million. Add to the financial losses the other metrics that were completely obliterated: industrial productivity fell over 50 per cent and in the early 1930s the unemployment rate rose as high as 25 per cent. It's easy to see why such losses in tangible value became known as the Great Depression.

During the Great Depression President Franklin D Roosevelt proved to be skilled and successful in tackling the abysmal social hardships caused by fiscal incompetence. He led a charge of longer term policies with the three Rs: relief for the unemployed, recovery of the overall economy and reform of the financial system. These included considerations outside of merely fiscal thinking into environmental factors such as protecting soil erosion. Franklin D Roosevelt considered three pillars equally relevant (quantitative, qualitative and mental fortitude thinking):

> The test of our progress is not whether we add more abundance of those who have much: it is whether we provide enough for those who have too little.

> A nation that destroys its soil destroys itself. Forests are the lungs of our land, purifying the air and giving fresh strength to our people.

> Democracy cannot succeed unless those who express their choice are prepared to choose wisely. The real safeguard of democracy, therefore, is education.

It's a good job he did. Historians suggest at the peak of the Great Depression the entire globe stood at the precipice of falling into another period akin to the Dark Ages.

Greed is not good

You'd have thought we'd take on board this invitation for more serious fiscal management (both governments and corporates) as a result of the hardships and crises from mass recession or depression. Alas! Here again these systems remind us we're like useless babies, still bumbling in the cot and not as smart as baby elephants. Fast forward to the global financial crisis (GFC) of 2007–08.

The GFC could easily have been labelled the GFU given the global financial crisis was triggered by great f**k-ups from lessons not learned. The fast world of finance and highflying investment banking took the bad idea of lending way more cash than is covered in reserve and turned it into an ethos. Fiscal management became high-rolling gaming more likely found in casinos. What had once been a wrecking ball to the economy in the thirties became a standard roll of the dice, pursuing success, results and wealth.

The pressures of delivering tangible value synonymous with shareholder expectations, enticing commissions, remuneration and gaining power proved all too enticing. Global financial systems had become a rigged game: toxic, rotten to the core, even if not always deliberately so, favouring a few institutions as chief high rollers.

Convoluted bundled product offerings were graded and rated secure with 'triple-A scores' by the very mechanisms built to call them out on their bullshit and prevent such catastrophes. In reality they were about as valuable as, but less solid than, some of those earliest known tokens of pebbles and stone.

As the evolution continues we can no longer not know this: a bloody minded, singular, selfish focus on accumulating money, greed unleashes the negative side of tangible value as a terror to all.

Today it's estimated a nominal 2 per cent of 'token' exchanges are attributed to the likes of cash. It's estimated that credit cards, online banking, zeros and ones fleeting in microseconds around the globe and other various electronic activities account for 98 per cent of all monetary transactions in this digital era.

Crypto currencies, underpinned by block chain technologies, loom large as the latest 'token' for the common dollar. Crypto currencies tick the required boxes exceptionally well: harder to forge, durable, effortless to transport or carry, and no doubt soon to be more legitimised.

At least crypto, a currency, is conceptually easier to understand than many other financial and monetary instruments: stocks long and short, bonds, margin calls, equities, securities and a variety of interesting ways to structure entities, 'shell' companies or even tax gamification. All are used for the acquisition of tangible value wealth.

The moment governments fully embrace or approve such things as crypto tax payments or bank loans, the currency—one you can't even physically touch—will render even more useless the trinkets of coins jingling in your pockets or dirty paper soiled by germs and graffiti. It's bizarre really that tangible money is now almost completely invisible. At least the ethereal token is better than some of the older ones. Barrels of beer for murder! Oh dear. Crypto is more considerate of the environment too given there's not a whale's tooth in sight.

Appreciating money

Some people continue to hoard physical amounts of ye old precious metals that can't be eroded so easily. For the larger majority of the population, tangible value or wealth resides now in technological clouds. Floating numbers forming totality of assets, credits and debts. All of which play their part towards the overall tangible value or net worth at hand. Through these historical adaptations people's relationship with money has simultaneously changed dramatically.

You may have relatives among those gold and silver hoarders who'll recall the days of receiving a physical pay packet. A small brown envelope with their weekly salary folded or wedged inside. We have a different perspective or appreciation of tokens we don't actually physically hold or touch.

Easy access to all forms of cash fosters less appreciation of what it truly represents (we'll get to that shortly). Fewer hands on your tokens, when added to consumerism demanding more amid a race where materialism is perceived to be valued, is a recipe for disaster.

Many, myself included, concede to the temptation of blowing hard-earned *moolah* (Fijian for money) on what *Rich Dad, Poor Dad*'s author Robert Kiyosaki terms 'doodads': material possessions that are depreciating liabilities or things which take money away from your pocket, and don't add any value to your real world or feeling of self-worth.

My own doodad vices are rooted in acquiring experiences and a nice wardrobe of threads, with a particular penchant for tailored suits. It's perhaps a remnant from being on the road in Europe for 10 years living out of suitcases. With no home to speak of, a nice wardrobe constituted touchable tokens I could appreciate for some sense of stability amid the transient lifestyle. I also learned the true value of experiences and gained a healthy regard for lifelong learning and continual growth.

So when I marry these ideas together, spending money on expensive treats or experiences, they can be an investment as much as a doodad. There are many who'd doubtless agree that a continual pursuit to improve yourself is a smart use of money. In fact Robert Kiyosaki said, 'when you are young, work to learn, not to earn!' On the other hand financial gurus may tell you a taste for anything expensive for the hell of it is akin to falling for poor 'doodad' traps. Consider the following as a guide if you suspect you're slipping into its grips. Invest your money on things and experiences that:

- are authentically you
- genuinely add to increasing self-confidence or happiness
- are within a firm belief that 'bling don't mean thing!'

while simultaneously being mindful that

- you don't 'need to have it' in order to be confident or happy
- there's no underlying motivation to simply impress others
- it's not retail therapy as an escape from life challenges.

After all, life is for living. Just don't view material possessions as a basis of absolute tangible value or self-worth.

When you look closely at grounded, wealthy individuals, often they're the simplest dressed folks who don't feel the need to show off. They don't brag, compare or share the surface, aesthetic, commercial trappings of perceived success.

The danger these days in being somewhat disconnected from our tokens is we slip more easily into acquiring doodads of shallow frivolity. If you actually received physical pay packets, I wonder, would you drop thousands or live under credit in order to upgrade iterations of the latest smart phone? It's why that line in the Netflix movie *Laundromat* leaped out at me: 'Credit is an invention that meant you no longer needed to carry around ... bananas on slips of paper'.

Credit is bananas from the future.

Numbers, digits and easy access to credit somewhat diminish our respect as to what money truly gives you. A healthier relationship with money—the true power of tangible value in the token cause of money—is this: financial prosperity increases access to resources which, when treated with respect and wisdom, have the potential to fulfil our and others' base needs. With these burdens or worries diminished we have an easier path to personal growth and self-actualisation by way of two mechanisms:

- consistently feeling good
- consistently doing good.

Who you are is ultimately not determined by what you wear or what you have.

Your worth or ability to add value is not purely determined by how much you amass.

Your self-worth and value are determined by feeling secure, fulfilled and happy.

The tangible value you add is the positive, measurable impact you may have on the lives of others.

Rudyard Kipling offered sound advice in a dedicated portion of his classic poem, 'If':

If you can make one heap of all your winnings

And risk it on one turn of pitch-and-toss

And lose, and start again at your beginnings

And never breathe a word about your loss.

Sticking with my weakness for threads and style, a Cary Grant quote sums it up nicely: 'Let them see you first and not the suit. The suit should be secondary'.

The Bill & Melinda Gates Foundation, launched in 2000, is one of the largest private foundations for social philanthropy in the world. Warren Buffet, another well-known billionaire and philanthropist doubled the pot donating a large amount of his own fortune to the foundation. We'll hear more about them in detail in the chapter on service value. For now, here's a powerful nugget from someone who has successfully leveraged the power of tangible value, Bill Gates: 'I can understand wanting to have a million dollars, but once you get beyond a point, I have to tell you, it's the same hamburger'.

2. Percentages

Leonardo da Vinci's tracings known as Vitruvian Man are estimated to date around 1490. Their title comes from the works and ideas of the Roman architect Vitruvius.

Vitruvius, a civil and military engineer of the 1st century, likened the three essential qualities that any structure must exhibit—stability, utility and beauty—to being the same within nature. Vitruvius described the characteristic 'proportions of man'—a human body lying flat with hands and feet splayed—as being geometrically circumscribed to fit within both a square and a circle.

Da Vinci's curiosity translated the text from this thesis into the now famous tracings.

Da Vinci documented many of his own notebooks and scribblings, including ones related to Vitruvian Man, using mirror writing. To decipher da Vinci's handwritten records you have to reflect the calligraphy in a mirror.

Da Vinci likely used this cutting-edge wisdom of record keeping in part because of the nature of his methods. He had an interest in the dead, namely in dissecting cadavers—yes, you read right!

This gruesome work, which most people would find morbid or immoral, incited that divergent da Vinci mind further down the rabbit hole of human body dimensions.

His fascination with dissecting, studying and drawing what he saw fuelled a greater thirst for understanding the human anatomy in all its beauty, form and function.

From his findings da Vinci observed many consistencies—as suspected and suggested by Vitruvius—across all cadavers, irrespective of the decomposing individual's height, weight or general shape. This included ratio percentages such as:

- the length between the tip of the chin and the top of the forehead is one-tenth of body height
- the open hand, from wrist to the tip of the middle finger, is also one-tenth of body height
- the middle of the chest breast plate to the summit of the crown is one-quarter of body height
- the bottom of the chin to the underside of the nostrils is one-third the total height of the face
- the length of the foot is one-sixth of body height
- the length of the forearm is one-quarter of body height

- three lengths measuring the circumference of the head is equal to body height

- the arm span (as featured on Vitruvian Man) is pretty much 1:1 equal to body height.

Invite a few friends over and try it out for yourself. No! Hold on! I'm not suggesting you become a psycho like Hannibal Lecter, killing your mates or even keeping them living while you cut open the tops of their heads to peer into their brains. I mean you can do the same thing using your living bodies—a fun home experiment science class that could be done over a couple of wines. Cut up some lengths of string to experiment with and then get into a game of Twister, helping each other measure. Hell, go the full da Vinci: splay out on the floor, complete with circles and squares, and see how it all fits (maybe put your wine down first).

As Vitruvius suspected, there are many other patterns within the human body and broader fields of nature. Advanced scientific study has continued to build upon these, highlighting various symmetries, including:

- *bilateral (mirror):* a line down the body centre with two halves essentially equal

- *radial (rotational):* parts equally arranged around a central axis, like a starfish

- *translational and scaling (repeating patterns):* like unfurling ferns (New Zealand Koru art represents this).

All of these ratios, proportions too, are quantitative measures highlighting how much one value either contains or is contained within another. In the tangible value language of business we generally refer to these ratios and proportions using the more common term, percentages.

A bank is unlikely to tell you that the ratio or proportion gained per annum from your deposit will be equal to one-tenth, one-quarter or one-third. Instead, they'll advise you the interest is

10 per cent, 25 per cent or 33 per cent respectively. And by the way, if you happen to find any mainstream bank offering such great returns, put out a flyer and let everyone else know, will you?

Percentages are inherent within the cosmic of our own makeup and the fabric of the universe so it makes sense that it be one of the four primary measures of tangible value. That said, percentages can't be separated from another measure. If you were to go into a bank and be told you're getting 10 per cent returns, what is that based on? The amount deposited in the first place. Which leads us into the third important metric.

3. Numbers

Numbering systems, like money, have their own evolution and history. Different civilisations evolved countless ways of keeping track. Ancient civilisations like the Aztecs, Egyptians or Greeks used a common method of keeping tally with a series of symbols and marks.

The tallying systems worked, yet as quantities grew larger the trick was creating new symbols to represent higher volumes or amounts.

As the Roman Empire spread it took with it many of its feats, such as engineering, roads, wine and, of course, the Roman numeral system. The Romans used seven primary symbols: I, V, X, L, C, D and M. These represented the amounts of 1, 5, 10, 50, 100, 500 and 1000 respectively.

The system could be considered somewhat innovative in its simplification of symbols and method of use—notably that if a symbol of lower value appeared before a symbol of higher value it was to be deducted rather than added. To tally higher numbers they would then draw bars above specific symbols depending how many times they were to be considered as repeated. This didn't make the documentation of larger numbers any easier.

A different and smarter way of tallying numbers was through creating what we now know as a positional notation. The Aztecs, Babylonians and Chinese all documented such methods where their system of counting allowed fewer symbols, the amount each symbol represented being determined by its position in the tally.

By the 8th century Indian mathematicians had created an elegant, easy-to-understand solution that was based on positional notation using only symbols. These symbols were to become the basis of our modern-day decimal system using only 10 glyphs instead of dozens: 1, 2, 3, 4, 5, 6, 7, 8, 9, 0.

Through conquerors and trade merchants, this system of counting ultimately made its way from East to West, through Persian and Arabic realms and ultimately into Europe.

By the 15th century, what we now know as the Hindu-Arabic (often times simply called Arabic) number system had replaced its predecessor, the Roman numerals, as a standard system of counting. It was from its use in Europe that its influence would then ultimately spread around the world.

This was partially due to the adoption by mathematicians and scientists, who then discovered and unlocked other ratios of wonder locked within nature. One of these was their promotion by yet another Leonardo: Fibonacci.

Leonardo Fibonacci inspired way more than a sequence. The secret codes that carry his name could be found in beautiful patterns of nature hidden in plain sight: drone bee genealogy, pineapple rings, flower petals and the golden ratio (or divine proportion) being the aesthetically pleasing pattern in the arrangement and spirals of leaves.

The percentages (ratios and proportions) whose existence we marvel at are brought to life, easy to understand, through the elegance of numbers. Both percentages and numbers pervade many other aspects of our life. And if these tangible metrics are locked within the biological code and DNA inherent in almost all of nature, which they assuredly seem to be, that's a big enough clue to their overall importance.

I want you to specifically remember the number '150'. That's right: *one hundred and fifty.* We're going to come back to it in chapter 5.

A more appropriate tribute right now would perhaps be to say,, remember: *Ek sau pachas* or *Meye w kamshin* (Hindu and Arabic for '150').

Here's why. We live on a planet with 196 recognised countries. Among them are 180 recognised currencies (excluding crypto currencies) with the oldest in existence being the British pound and the strangest being the Turkish coco pops, in addition to the lira. Oh yeah, didn't I tell you? The tasty chocolate crackling cereal was another form of bartering tokens on Contiki tours. A couple of boxes usually proved enough to procure the final border release signature allowing the coach to exit Turkey on the way into Bulgaria. On one crossing, with stocks running low, I offered three packs of Weet-Bix. The machine-gun-holding guard abruptly threw them back at me and cheekily muttered three words: 'No. Coco Pops'.

Despite the historical diversification of tokens turned into currencies, or even language, it's conversely curious that the symbols and mechanisms for measuring the metrics of percentages and numbers are pretty much universally adopted.

Numbers, along with proportions and percentages, increasing or decreasing, play a significant role in the measured success of every business or home budget on the planet. We use numbers in everyday transactions to explain something simply or to ask for what it is we seek. That one extra-large coffee you may require to kick start your day is easier to say than drawing up a tally symbol. Those spreadsheets and reports you need to break down and make sense of are far easier with 10 glyphs and decimal points rather than complicated lines of Roman numerals further convoluted by horizontal repetitive bars.

In an early draft of a book of my experiences from the Contiki days, a working title was *Fifty-one plus two*. The reason for this was that it's a simple way of explaining the breakdown of numbers in a tour group. The first number, 51, represented the number of passengers on tour. The second number, 2, represented the number of road crew.

Numbers filled my every day: documenting and counting the numbers of passengers attending each unique excursion, numbers for hotel rooms and allocations, numbers translated into multiple currencies. Perhaps the most common pastime was the daily head counts! Every travel day you'd be performing a head count, then you'd double check it, to make sure you didn't leave someone stranded in a service stop somewhere on a motorway. In a city, after letting the group loose for their free time, you'd reconvene at a meeting point and perform headcounts before continuing the walking tour or heading to the coach pick-up point. No easy feat in busy summer crowds with people constantly moving around. You'd try to find a vantage point a few steps higher, and coerce static cooperation from your group.

I think the worst head count in my tour history happened in Brindisi. (Italians are notorious for changing processes or systems on a whim.) We were heading by ferry to Greece. At this particular passport office, as a tour leader, you might arrive alone, having collected everyone's individual passports because the last time you were here that's what you were asked to do. The officers on duty would then send you back to get each individual passenger. On other occasions, covering your bases, you'd have every passenger come with you, at which point the officer on duty would say, no, you as the guide just collect all the passports from the passengers and bring them to me. It was always hit and miss.

I'd learned it was a safer bet to just have passengers with me regardless. We arrived at the passport office to absolute chaos. I think a prior ferry must have been cancelled. The volume of people scrambling to be processed was like the worst fighting crowds you might envisage at department store Boxing Day sales.

I don't know how, but one of the guards on duty picked me for a tour guide and decided on this occasion I should collect the passports from my people and process them alone. He yelled this instruction at me. A few people in my group heard the instruction and repeated it, yelling aloud 'everyone give your passports to Mark!'

I was on the verge of yelling 'No, don't do that just yet', when passports began hitting my head, landing on the floor and flying past my face. It was complete mayhem and it wasn't just my passengers who were trying to get their passports into my hands. Half an hour later I was still trying to make sense of the 63 passports I'd collected. Quite an achievement having only 51 plus two on board!

Numbers and percentages play a significant part of our daily life. Yet, as important as they are, it's perhaps the fourth tangible measure that I find a greater priority: time. It's one considered by science to be merely an illusion allowing us each to make better sense of our worlds. The construct of time has inspired thousands of firmly fixed clichés. I can't affirm as a scientist decidedly either way whether 'time waits for no man' or not. But I can attest that ferries running to Greece out of Brindisi don't!

4. Time

Michelangelo di Lodovico Buonarroti Simoni, more simply known as Michelangelo, is another legendary Italian artistic figure at the time of the Renaissance. Like Leonardo da Vinci he too mastered multiple mediums of artistic expression: carpentry, architecture, sculpting and a broad range of methodologies for painting, even though he held them in far lower regard.

Pope Julius II commissioned Michelangelo for a variety of projects in the Vatican, among them remodelling the building of a papal tomb. One such project was the task of painting the ceiling of the great Sistine Chapel in the Apostolic Palace. Michelangelo had little hunger or even willingness for the task. In fact there's a story suggesting that architect Donato Bramante convinced the pope to commission Michelangelo out of spite or envy for Michelangelo's involvement in the work on the tombs.

Nevertheless, Michelangelo invested four years of his life on his vision for the ceiling. This included constructing innovative scaffolding and even breaking away from time-tested traditions regarding fresco paintings in order to complete the mesmerising work we now marvel at.

He then painted a second sizeable fresco on the chapel wall: 'The Last Judgement'. This body of work, equally as fascinating, consumed a further four years of his life. That's eight years dedicated to mediums he didn't particularly rank as important. He saw this investment of time as valuable though, as it allowed him access to the projects that were his ultimate aim.

The monumental volume of lifetime works he created is prodigious. Had he left only a single work, he'd likely still be immortalised; yet he, like other Renaissance figures, left a breathtaking catalogue of creativity. He also acts as a reminder of the power of what can be achieved when we double down our investment of time with our best efforts—even where it might involve tasks that are not preferred.

Not even the best photography or videography, both of which are frowned upon in the sanctity of the Sistine Chapel anyway, do complete justice to the works. Seeing these creations with your own two eyes, head spinning or with an aching neck straining to look upwards, helps appreciate the artistry, scale, challenges and commitment of the masterful artist.

Rome was a frequent destination on many of my Contiki itineraries. Rome's two most popular tourist attractions are the Colosseum (a perfect paganistic symbol of power and degradation given it was central to a civilisation credited with orgies and worshipping many gods) and of course, the Vatican Museum, with its many treasures.

Lines for visiting the Vatican City begin to form in the early hours of the morning. It's not unusual to arrive sometime after 8 am to already find a queue wrapped halfway around the 3.2 kilometres of wall that make up the independent state.

I'd frequently walk my groups past these queues, at which point the passengers would peer in disbelief or despair at the thought of joining the waiting ranks, especially if it was in the heat of summer.

A benefit of being on the tour was we'd already pre-booked a local guide. This meant earlier access via a group entry into the Vatican Museum itself. The moment guests realised they'd be skipping the queues with this early entry coup, those same deflated faces would light up into smiles. It was as if I'd just finished putting the last lick of paint on the frescoes that very morning for them to enjoy. And why?

Because they intrinsically knew the value of this fourth metric—time—and appreciated the gift of time to do things other than stand in queues.

As pretty-much all biographies from successful entrepreneurs attest, you can make money and you can just as easily lose money. Even if a business fails, the time invested is still of use, provided you take away some learnings. You can make and lose friends. Invariably, as you learn and grow, people will drift in and out of the dance that is your life. But every second spent ... well, that's an irreplaceable moment of potential that's gone.

To some degree then a watch is like a symbolic token of the value of time it represents: a beautiful, decorative tangible reminder — not a doodad — to protect your most precious commodity. Choose and act wisely with how you make your investments. Be consciously selective with how, who and what you invest your time in.

Time is another of the patterns of measurable metrics already referenced as inherent across nature (bilateral, radial, translational)—for example the rhythmic pattern changes in time, music, sound or the ocean's waves.

Consider that an average human life spans over 155 billion seconds, give or take a few hundred million. Then imagine if each second directly translated to a dollar amount: the dollar in question being either financial or, more importantly, personal fulfillment and a feeling of value and self-worth. How keen would you be to ensure banking or investing your time wisely so as to reap the significant reward of what Albert Einstein described as the eighth wonder of the world: compound interest?

A life extraordinary—a life of real value and worth—is a life comprising billions of seemingly singular, spontaneous, random moments sculpted and fused together with passion and purpose. Put another way, extraordinary people such as Michelangelo add value to the world, leaving legacies. They're ordinary individuals, leveraging their innate natural talents to compound their time interestingly through conscious choices and actions.

Time is the one thing that you spend and once it's gone you don't get back. That's reason enough to heed the Italian romantic-sounding expression:

Tratta il tempo come fosse il tuo migliore amante!

Treat time like a most precious lover!

The tangible value of dollars, numbers and percentages, compounded with time, truly represent a path to feeling both freedom and fulfillment. I remember watching an interview some years ago with Sir Terry Pratchett (the famous hat-wearing author of 41 Discworld fantasy novels) where he cites enormous gratitude for the success of his books. Not for the fame or money alone but because they afforded him an opportunity to pay others to do things they wanted to do that Pratchett himself either didn't wish or have the talent to do himself.

Tangible value
Tools, tips and self-reflEQtion

Putting off pressures or stresses around money or time doesn't make them go away. This seems to be one of my own Achilles heels! Being obsessed with money to secure material trappings of success equally isn't healthy. This, on the other hand, is far from my own frivolous manner, more frequently playing out by living in the moment of experiences or through generosity to others.

It's also a good idea to do what any leader or business might: take a snapshot and benchmark measurable starting points. Use the same ones to revert back to as periodic check-ins to celebrate aspirational gains or adjust your actions—for example gym results or financial savings.

Tangible value works best in harmony with all the other values. To isolate it is to risk falling for the negative side of its allure. Be mindful to blend any laser focus towards tangible value by conducting yourself in a manner of high ethics and authenticity. Apply your personal values, skills and traits to compound the power of each of the metrics.

Here are some quick tips to provoke more calculated thought, but remember to listen to other ideas unleashed by your own intuition.

What is my relationship with money?

Identify limiting beliefs or negative thought patterns in relation to finances.

Ask yourself, 'Where did these come from?' Where did you learn them?

Set actions to 'reframe' your thinking.

Budget essential expenses

If you're feeling stressed out about personal or household bills, set a plan to get them under heel. Conduct a weekly/monthly/annual budget of expenses. If this is an Achilles heel for you, don't be shy in seeking help. The book *Spenditude* by Paul Gordon and Janine Robertson offers further depth and insights. It shows you how to tackle habits and behaviours to drive your spending, allowing financial security while living the life you want.

Eliminate retail non-therapy or minimise the doodads

Race less to the checkouts! Ask, 'Why am I really wanting to get this?' If the answers are merely masks to help you feel good, reconsider the purchase. Rather, invest in items and brainpower, like continual learning that will serve a deeper fulfillment which will last for a longer time.

Be where you are

When you're with friends, family or clients respect and value the time. Put away your phone, stay off other technology, simply be where you are. If you're making a choice to be present, then embrace the decision. Cave less to the temptation of FOMO or short-term, temporary, dopamine feedback loops that act as a quick artificial fix towards fulfillment.

Claim back your time

Where are you investing or spending the majority of your time? Do you even really know? Many people are surprised at the results of any stocktake. Deepak Chopra wrote a bestselling book on a single flight (*The Seven Spiritual Laws of Success*) while others tootled the time away on in-flight entertainment. Consider assessing your own typical day/week/month.

Protect your calendar and clock

If you're feeling there's not enough hours in the day, identify the priorities and allocate blocks of time. Another of my Achilles heels is too strong a focus on business, even though I enjoy it. Make sure to include time-out for leisure. A focus on quantity, quality and mental attitude (as Roosevelt recommended) may alleviate stresses or impending depressions.

Ask better tangible value questions of others

Don't assume because you're driven by the dollar others are too. Learn to ask strategic questions to uncover the important metrics in their world. Then be interested in listening to the answers. This allows you, professionally or personally, to add or align real value.

3

Emotional value

Make me feel it

American poet Maya Angelou wrote, 'I've learnt that people will forget what you said, people may forget what you did, but people will never forget how you made them feel'.

Elisabeth Kübler-Ross, a Swiss-American psychiatrist, is best remembered for groundbreaking research on near-death experiences and studies with the terminally ill. Peeking back through life to a distant cradle with one foot in the grave affords a unique perspective of value.

Her book *On Death and Dying*, released in 1969, was and remains a body of work considered cutting edge and controversial. She broke ground by describing people's emotions and regrets when facing death by way of her five stages of grief model: denial, anger, bargaining, depression and acceptance.

Her son, Ken Ross, founder of the Elisabeth Kübler-Ross Foundation, also pursued a career in palliative care. He shared in a variety of interviews and articles several incidents where his mother faced death threats. Their family home was even burned down, twice, as a result of her support for children living with AIDS.

Her famous model was, as Ross points out, never intended as complete or linear. The model prised open important dialogues. It wasn't to be interpreted as a black and white playbook pondering mortality. The stages within the model helped better contextualise and appreciate the one-way destination each of us face. Up to that point it was little discussed and perhaps, with little empirical tangible data, even misunderstood.

The mainstream model drafted and released was simplified to a five-stage version. When working in-depth with professionals, the expanded theoretical version encompassed 10 to 13 stages. This included others from the positive-feeling end of the spectrum, such as hope.

Any suggested processes for handling an impending face-to-face meeting with death, pondering the realities of mortality like the layers of behaviour and life experiences that shape or define us, are unique. They must be. The course of contemplation of the value or meaning of life can't be scripted or laid out as neat sequential measures of ingredients and instructions in a cookbook. Even the best recipes additionally have variations in portions or order of progression.

Curiously enough, Ken Ross shared that when his mother, incapacitated through a series of strokes, faced her own mortality she seemed to remain stuck in one stage of her own simplified model: anger for not being able to appreciate or enjoy a peaceful retirement. Even on our deathbed we may be reminded that life remains, until our last breath, a journey of continual learning, unlearning and relearning no matter how self-actualised or masterful we have become.

If we consolidate an approach to the idea of value through the lens of Elisabeth Kübler-Ross in the style of 'Benjamin Button', working backwards grave to cradle, we tap into a fuller appreciation of this critical element. When a life is reviewed through the rear-view mirror of reflection, then the emotional impacts of some of those situations, like passing objects, appear up close.

Your history is your memory. Your history isn't the photos of your past. Without memory you have no history. The mind's eye, the curator of your personal library, also happens to be a pretty sophisticated camera. It's far superior to the best offering of any smart phone. A million selfies will pale when matched against the mind's eye reliving experiences from your past. The more you live fully in each passing moment, fully submerged, the richer the archives recalled when recounting your past.

Your memory has a tendency to romanticise. Within the science of neuroplasticity we are educated on how memories are formed and recalled. Our brains have an ability to exaggerate or diminish details and textures from previous life experiences. The low points or summits from mountains faced or conquered. Yet even where particulars are embellished, your memory reminds faithfully the accurate gamut of moods that were anchored at the time. A range of emotions well beyond five, a result of all the tears, smiles, joys, sadness, hopes, regrets, optimism or despair.

I'm a bit of a movie buff. I especially love the classics. Audrey Hepburn [sigh]. The American Film Institute has a list of its top 100 all-time great movies. At the top of this list sits the 1941 Orson Welles classic *Citizen Kane*. The two-hour-long RKO production was almost prevented from release given the fiction was seen to be partially, not so subtly, based on the life of newspaper magnate William Randolph Hearst. The film unravels the life of its fictional lead character, Charles Foster Kane.

* *Spoiler alert*: if you feel you'd like to watch the movie having never seen it, skip the next paragraph.

* * *

* *Double spoiler alert*: seriously, last chance; skip the next couple of paragraphs if you want to know nothing!

'Rosebud' is the last word muttered from his lips as Foster Kane takes his final breath. The film's narrative then follows the enquiries of a journalist, Jerry Thompson, who's trying to get the root of what the word 'Rosebud' actually meant.

He tracks down those who knew Foster Kane, who had schooled him, worked with him, even married or lived with him. We see Charles Foster Kane as a child playing in the snow on his sled and we see him sent away to be schooled and mentored by a guardian after his mother has come into a cash windfall, the result of a goldrush. Foster Kane begins adulthood as a man of ideological social awareness, fairness and truth. Later he yields a ruthless unbending nature of power without compromise. We see snippets of his life, happily married to affairs and scandal. The accumulation of massive wealth even in spite of failed ambition to an ultimate recluse with a handful of precious memories. One above all others especially, the journalist discovers, reminds him of something. After wrecking a room in anger he's calmed by a single recollection after glimpsing into a snow globe. It's the only other time anyone has heard him mutter the word 'Rosebud'. What was calming about the snow globe and what did it mean?

Absolute final spoiler alert: the next paragraph will be annoying if you're going to watch the film. Don't hate on me.

The secret of that final dying word, 'Rosebud', remains undiscovered by the reporter. When his estate is being sold, some items are discarded and destroyed. A worthless snow sled is thrown into the fires. As the heat disintegrates the aged layers of dust, dirt and paint the word 'Rosebud', the name of his childhood sled, is revealed to the viewer. It turns out the innocent, carefree memories of the playful child version of Foster Kane reminded him of happiness before the adult-version layers of the business magnate got in the way and tainted simple joys.

** *Spoiler alert complete!* You're safe now! All you need to know is this: the movie *Citizen Kane* is a perfect example, reiterating the value of a life journey, cradle to grave, for discovering the emotions and moods that weave together a rich tapestry.

In my search I've found scores of descriptions people use that fall into this particular element of value. All can be simplified to one fundamental concept. Everything we want to be, do or have in this life is because the being, doing or having of it we believe will make us feel good.

Emotional value in a nutshell

Don't wait until you're dying to discover the practical application of four significant causes — or layers — that illuminate emotional value. They help amass in both feeling and fortune a life far more gratifying.

1. The power of storytelling
2. Sensory experience
3. Personalisation: the 'wow' factor
4. Leaps in creative faith: innovation

1. The power of storytelling

I'm going to present you an item, a pitch if you will, in two different ways. For each one, take a pause, ponder and swiftly decide a figure value (a dollar amount) you deem it to be worth. The item in question is a toy bear. Are you ready for your first pitch and valuation? Let me tell you about the bear...

This bear is over 100 years old.

The bear has had six previous owners.

The bear has moveable arms and legs.

When you tip the bear gently upside down, then gradually straighten it, the bear will make the sound of a growl: a kind of muffled 'moo'.

Now pause for a moment and mentally select or write down a dollar figure for the bear. Okay, do you have it? Anchor it for a couple of minutes in your memory.

Are you ready for your second pitch and valuation? Yes?

Good. We'll get back to the bear in a moment.

First I need to tell you about Margarete. I often discuss her relative to strength and resilience of character.

Margarete, you see, was born in Giengen, Germany, in 1847. At 18 months she suffered a high fever resulting in paralysis of her legs and causing constant severe pain in her right arm, a condition later diagnosed as polio. Yet, despite this dire prognosis Margarete had a natural zest and fought to lead a normal life.

At age 15 Margarete taught herself to sew and began working part time in a dressmaking shop run by her sisters. By age 17 she became a fully trained, competent seamstress, which gave her the confidence (feeling of self-sufficiency or self-worth) to ultimately venture into business on her own creating and trading mostly clothing and general household items. She invested her first earnings into securing sewing machines. The pain in her right arm led to her innovatively turning the machines around in order to maximise her comfort and efficiency.

It was several years later that Margarete stumbled on patterns for a small elephant. It sparked her creativity to repurpose them into fabric elephant toys and pincushions for kids. She took a few thousand to the nearby fair in Leipzig where they sold like hot cakes. So Margarete began designing and manufacturing a variety of other animals as toys. Then, in 1897, her nephew Richard had an idea for a new line: 'PB55'.

(Now hold that thought for a moment as we slice and dice this narrative in the quirky style of a Tarantino movie script: let's skip across the globe quickly for a moment to absorb another short, yet very important, scene.)

Meanwhile ...

Over in the United States the sitting president attended a hunting trip where he was asked to shoot an animal tethered to a tree. Lowering his rifle, the leader refused to do so on the grounds that it was inhumane. It could be considered an out-of-character choice as the well-loved president in question was hardly an animal rights conservationist given the number of fine beasts that otherwise fell to the crack of his rifle. Yet in this instance, thinking it unfair and unsportsmanlike that the beast in question was tethered, the act of humanity earned President Theodore Roosevelt a nickname. Theodore Roosevelt hated the moniker, Teddy. Yet it was one destined to become known around the world.

(Tarantino quick-scene complete!)

Back in Germany ...

Margarete was initially a little sceptical of her nephew's 'PB55' idea, yet she agreed to test the previously fortuitous markets at the Leipzig toy fair in 1903. An American businessman stumbled on the toy animal made from dyeable plush mohair. He placed an initial order in the thousands, thus significantly opening channels for international distribution. He then gained permission from Roosevelt to name the bears 'teddy bears' and from 1906 onwards, the toy was sold under the new name. The toy animal was the very same growling animal Roosevelt had humanely saved.

Margarete's last name was Steiff. Steiff bears are considered to be the original teddy bears. What's more, Steiff bears have become highly collectible, in part thanks to another smart decision dating back to 1904. Franz, another of Margarete's nephews working in the business, came up with the idea of trademarking the toys using the iconic 'Knopf-im-Ohr' ('button-in-ear') trademark to ward off the copycats and fakes attempting to break into the market.

Margarete's international trade exploded her business. By the time of her death in 1909, aged 61, Steiff was trading approximately two million toys globally. Elephants had also expanded into an array of cuddly animals that could walk, crawl, climb, swim, jump or fly.

Margarete, through her tenacity, passion, resilience and creativity, had built a company that still stands today, as solid and concrete as her toys were soft. What's more, she did so with the company's motto remaining core to their ethos: *Only the best is good enough for children.*

So now let's come back to that pitch, shall we? You're now ready for your second valuation. Let me now tell you about the bear...

The bear is over 100 years old. The reason the bear is over 100 years old is because it's an original Steiff, a quite rare early version, within the first few years of production.

The bear has had six previous owners. The reason it's only had six previous owners is because generally such items are difficult to come by, available only via special auction, private purchase or through effort and diligence in research or knowing where to go.

The bear has moveable arms and moveable legs. Consider the flexible joints a lovely design component gifted to Steiff toys, a luxury Margarete didn't easily have herself, given her confinement to a wheelchair and the lifelong discomfort in her limbs.

When you tip the bear gently upside down, then straighten it again gradually, the bear will make the sound of a growl, a kind of muffled 'moo'. It may be considered a symbolic gesture, under presidential pardon, of the untethered animal's freedom cry.

So, pause again for a moment and mentally select or write down a second dollar figure for the bear. Okay, do you have it? What's the number, the dollar figure?

How does that perception of value rate in comparison to your first dollar figure?

The first pitch and valuation, being based merely on 'tangible value' facts (the year, number of owners, facts in relation to essential features) frequently draws a majority of responses ranging from $5 to $500 with some consideration given to its potential antiquity.

Generally speaking, I've found over 80 per cent of people consistently increase their value perception the second time around. Often times significantly so! The majority of responses will range between $1000 and $100000 on this second bout after initial perceptions of only a few dollars. Which is surely a more delicious ambiguity than that IQ benchmark known as borderline!

There are also those who retain their perception of value as the same between versions 1 and 2. Nothing changes. Which is also perfect because, let's face it, at the end of the day the item in question is a cuddly toy.

Someone who looks at tangible value preferring solid investments of bricks and mortar may not perceive the value of a stuffed animal in the same light.

And the point really is this. I deliberately use the quirky example of a teddy bear because the unlikeness of its impact highlights magnificently a fantastic lesson to be learned. You may get a sense from the style of my writing I've always been fascinated by history. Adding in a thirst to learn, I was always curious to investigate more.

I used to share the Steiff story with Contiki travellers when in Germany. Unless they already knew Steiff or collected them, only a minimum number of tourists found it relevant, or paid attention during my first pitch. However, the moment I shared the full background, I noticed a significantly greater number of people would be attentive or indeed purchase a Steiff as a souvenir. I anchored the philosophy and have used it ever since.

A super power to shift perspectives

So now imagine the same principle applied to a more significant community, product or philanthropic idea. Imagine if you mastered the same skill and used it powerfully to educate communities, decision makers or even people with greater positions of power and influence in industry, government or developing countries? What might the impact be? You may never convert or expand everyone's perception of value but, as with the bear, if you chip away each time, helping 80 per cent of people, 50 per cent even, adapt their thinking, what might be the results in these gains?

And what is the magic ingredient that helped shift perspective between the first and second versions of that pitch? Whisper it aloud.

Most people will say 'the story'. Storytelling is a powerful nucleus in conversations, with the potential to move mountains of closed-minded obstinance.

In actuality all four layers of emotional value were at play, however storytelling stands out more than the others.

In all aspects of our personal lives we are drawn or repelled by the quality of the narrative. The books we read, the movies we view or the yarns we share with friends in social settings. All pull us in or push us away.

No matter whether fact or fiction, embellished or improvised, lofty aspirations or raw grounded reality, we love stories. The better they're brought to life, through texture and rich descriptions engaging all our senses, the harder it is to resist being drawn into the colour of their light.

Stories educate and inspire collaboration or a fresh perspective. Equally they may be used as weapons or defensive walls to fracture and divide. Media ply your feed with stories vying for the time of your precious attention in order to achieve the tangible value metric of ratings.

Stories are so engrained in our psyche there are even potential formulas, archetypal themes. We can build, weave or mix and match narratives around in order to appeal to our audience:

1. Tragedy or tear-jerking heartbreak
2. Rags to riches

3. Mystery: what the hell is going on?

4. A quest for some kind of treasure

5. Anecdotal comedies or a calamity of laughable errors

6. Overcoming the monster to create a brave new world

7. Romance to find the ultimate prize of true love.

All provoke emotional responses and memory on the seesaw of human emotion weighted on one end with love and the counterbalance appeal of fear.

Metaphorical stories, chosen wisely, have the power to untangle or reconsider fixed mindsets or invoke open-mindedness to something new.

And let's not forget that human beings are renewing each day their collective personal value as all experiences are churned through their mind's cogs as meaning-making machines. Whether you like it or not, people are interpreting everything you're sharing against their own two logs of experience: inner dialogue and life catalogue.

No-one, not even the Dalai Lama, has enough words or wisdom to tell anyone what they should think. People make those decisions for themselves. Trying to impress value, values or importance onto another through autocratic rule or demand is doomed to fail. If you doubt it, try telling a vegetarian they should eat a steak. The same is true for all polarised viewpoints. Values and beliefs make that task virtually impossible.

Yet somehow amid this understanding of storytelling some bright sparks (likely with a strong focus on tangible value) latched onto an idea that graphs and data analysis alone do the same job. PowerPoint and spreadsheets! Pleeeasse!

They fail to see that while data is critically important the analysis points are like a dot-to-dot drawing. Sometimes the image may be obvious before pen touches paper. Other times the story is hidden and far more complex to perceive. Story is what breathes life to any numbers. When we look at nature we don't see the code of Fibonacci sequences locked in those leaves; we're too busy appreciating the golden ratio of the beautiful unfurling of ferns. Stories give shape, form and context to all facts and data. The story is what makes it compelling.

Storytelling, especially in business, is often delivered as a data download or cold, plain facts. That's an approach used to close an open and shut case in a legal courtroom. Even lawyers know it doesn't take away the importance of provoking emotion.

That's what I'd call a feature dump rather than the story. A dump is a pile of horse manure: that's the feature. It's literally shit. The right kind of manure, well spread where necessary, turns rich fields of crops for harvest: that's the story. That's the gold.

Wisely selected stories with strong links of relevancy to all perspectives create opportunity for engagement.

There are a few things hardwired into human existence that require little teaching to know their importance. For example, dancing wildly, even without rhythm, around a fire is something everyone can do. So is participation in the power of storytelling.

Novelist Bryce Courtenay once simplified our world in a short, sweeping statement to two types of people: masterful storytellers and eager cross-legged listeners.

We are both. In some fields we are the storytellers. If we can master the power of delivering captivating narratives we draw our audience in. Without telling them they must do anything the seeds we plant influence rich crops and valuable, tangible results. In other fields we are the cross-legged listeners. Even in this capacity it's important to be present. Listening to stories attentively means we pluck out and discard the wasteful weeds and water only seeds of rich quality crops we wish to see grow.

2. Sensory experience

We experience our entire world through all faculties. Along with the five traditional ones of smell, sight, sound, touch and taste, some mediums of science and neurologists believe they have identified an additional four and potentially even 16.

The sense of balance (otherwise known as proprioception) and the sense of knowing where your body parts are in relation to each other are two of them. I guess they must be valid. I've seen many informal experiments on Contiki tours and at office Christmas parties where these capacities are both completely diminished. After being exposed to alcohol, test subjects completely forget where their mouths are, poking cups into their noses or eyes, flopping around all over the place like rag dolls.

The muscles focusing your eyes work out around 100 000 times a day: the equivalent exertion in power to around a 80-kilometre hike. Human eyes are so sensitive that if you had 20/20 vision and the earth was flat you'd pick out a flickering candle at night as far away as 50 kilometres.

Each of those bright sophisticated eyes contains over two million working parts. They can distinguish around seven million subtle variations in hues.

Some of us seem to value this sense more than others. Colour appreciation champions are easy to pick. They'll accurately correct your assessment of light purple as being lilac. Or they shake their heads at your incapacity to recognise magenta as you refer to it as dark pink. I've got friends so sophisticated in this valuable intelligence they educate me on the difference between egg shell, alabaster, parchment and lace. I sometimes find myself interrupting them to explain my confusion. A moment earlier when describing a pair of runners I thought as white they'd somehow moved on talking about salt, egg shell or rice. I thought we'd stopped discussing footwear and colours completely moving on instead to food. Half an hour later we'll stumble into the same awkward predicament shopping for boots. While I think the items being pondered are tan, the descriptions of granola, shortbread or latte make me think they want to take a coffee break.

You'll likely salivate enough in a lifetime to fill two Olympic-size swimming pools. Some may find their mouths watering more than others. Especially those with deftness for delving into the delicious diversification and subtle undertones of the five essential tastes: sweet, sour, salt, bitter and umami. These gustatory guardians may also add pungent, stringent or delish to their descriptive ranges. The thousands of taste buds we all have regenerate in cycles as little as every 10 days. Which possibly explains the production of so much spit. It might act in part as lubrication to keep our oral engineering so optimal.

Senses of taste and smell are like close siblings. They have so much fun together a majority of the time. But watch out! Each has a tendency to annoy the crap out of the other when not behaving their best. Both also serve as avenues to the lungs.

The nose is the main boulevard for breathing, with the mouth a secondary thoroughfare. Both act like safety officers distinguishing dangerous toxins: smoke, deadly berries and the likes. The human nose is possibly the best air filter on the planet, blocking germs, capturing potential viruses and moderating air temperature before allowing it to pass and enter the lungs.

The nose and the ears, on the other hand, are more like distant cousins. They have a strange connection as predominant features that continue to grow with age.

In addition to their obvious purpose of listening, our ears play a vital role in our sense of balance. Our hearing may not be as advanced as that of canine family members or other animals, but we can hear frequencies from as low as 20 Hertz up to 20000 Hertz. For better appreciation, let's analyse this range in the context of mothers. At the lower end mums, even when fast asleep, will be alerted to the slightest tiptoeing of naughty toddlers creeping from beds in the middle of the night. In the mid range they will decipher every word whispered by scheming teenagers even beyond the halls and closed bedroom doors. At the upper end they can endure loud heavy metal music in short bouts without too much damage. Just long enough to tell you to turn the darn thing down! While perhaps less impressive in stats than other sensing parts, perhaps the ears' most unique value proposition is that of being self-cleaning. Which is pretty impressive given they cope with all that wax protecting us from dirt, muck and other irritants.

The human finger can feel objects as small as 13 nanometres. To translate this, imagine if your finger were the size of the earth. You'd still be able to delineate the difference in items as small as houses and cars. This sense of touch is credited as the most developed in babies and infants.

This early subtle mastery in touch generally remains a primary one throughout life. Look at how we continue to interact with our world. Handshakes, high-fives, head pats, cuddles and group hugs. Anthropologist Robin Dunbar (about whom we'll hear more later) relates its importance to quality communication.

We all know the slightest touch can trigger an irk of yukkiness, a cautionary signal you may also feel in the gut when something's not quite right. A polite gesture can stimulate a sense of neutrality or set silent boundaries that you've just been placed in the friend zone. A different innocent caress on the other hand may also unleash exciting electrical chemistry, sending the brain into meltdown and turning you to mush. A heartfelt touch, especially in conjunction with silent eye contact, says 'I love you' far deeper than any number of words or creative expression. Touch can be calming, supportive and set social standards. It's long been known in the animal kingdom that touch is essential for emotional development and critical skills in order to blend with the herd, flock or pack. We know human babies crave to be nurtured. Given how useless and daft they otherwise are we love them for this cute itching hunger to be hugged.

All five primary senses are considered common although some people may be disadvantaged through genetics or disability. Even then they'll frequently develop the others to be far more acute to compensate any absence. We experience our world through all the senses at our disposal then file the captured memories as archives with attachments of emotions and moods.

It's why salespeople usher you to look and climb inside the sexy body of a new car, smell the leather, clutch the wheel, then take it for a test drive to feel its handling. The sensory overload makes the car so appealing you may even want to lick it. It's why the café or bakery hands out samples on the street. It's why tailors want you to run your fingers over textures. It's why designers want you to compare colour cards. Well, either that or just for kicks so they've got fun stories to share later with friends about the dopey customer who couldn't distinguish the difference between peach and apricot.

The more we connect with our senses (or engage those of others) the easier it is for many precious subtleties so often otherwise missed to become magnified. Engaging the senses ignites greater appreciation of both our inner and external worlds.

3. Personalisation: the 'wow' factor

Some elements of my work require large amounts of energy, including a lot being drained via intellectual muscle. You may be surprised how much is required to consistently create content to engage audiences from the stage. There are times I need to get out of my head and into my body. The obvious outlet includes physical activity like training at the gym. A part of me has always enjoyed creative artistic pursuits too: drawing, painting and even dabbling in handcrafts. Specifically hand weaving and making dreamcatchers.

There's a lovely story concerning the origin of dreamcatchers amid the Ojibwe tribe, one of the largest American-Indian tribes. In their tradition, one of their spiritual leaders was called Spider Woman. It was believed she communicated messages to the tribes, including all the toddlers in their cradles. When the kin was located in a single geographical area this was easy. As the tribe grew and dispersed throughout the entire continent of North America it was said to be more difficult for Spider Woman to visit them all. The American-Indians believed the night air was full of dreams: the good, the bad and the downright ugly. And given the difficulty the sleeping toddlers had in deciphering these messages, the mothers and grandmothers of the tribes decided to help out. So they began weaving dreamcatchers to help Spider Woman communicate her messages with ease and clarity. By hanging a dreamcatcher above their sleeping heads, the young could purify their dreams. The nightmares were caught in the net while the sweet ones dripped down the feathers into their subconscious. So the sleeping child would only go into action in their waking life with their positive dreams driving their choices.

Each element of the traditional dreamcatcher serves a powerfully symbolic purpose. The round hoop represents the movement of the sun and the moon. It was believed that nightmares were born in the dark and destroyed in the light, so the hoop's web would catch the nightmares and detain them until the sun's rays could destroy them. The sweet dreams were allowed to flow freely to the sleeping person to become fuel for creativity unencumbered by harmful subconscious imagery from nightmares. Traditional dreamcatchers were made from natural, biodegradable materials, like willows for the hoops, twine or vine for the woven web, and real feathers found on the ground. The idea was for a child's dreamcatcher to degrade over time so by the time they reached adulthood, their childish fears and desires had disintegrated and returned to the earth.

It was in the 20th century that the use of dreamcatchers was made accessible outside the realms of American-Indian tradition. I'm aware that making dreamcatchers could be considered as culturally disrespectful given I'm not from an American-Indian tribe. However, my dreamcatchers are always made as gifts and not for commercial gain.

Working in the field of human development, behaviour and potential I find this an alluring philosophy. I also find the hand making of dreamcatchers quite therapeutic at times. A tactile creative outlet that is very different from the mental energy and focus it takes to build keynote and development-program content. I was making dreamcatchers long before I realised my brand initials, MC, were slap-bang in the middle. And so my adapted versions became dreaMCatchers.

Each dreaMCatcher is made for a particular owner or inspired theme through carefully chosen colours and charms, including precious and semi-precious stones. They can take anywhere from two to eight hours to build, depending on the size and complexity. While I've improved my methods over time, a little like dabbling with paints, I'm no natural web weaver. They can be tricky to make. Then again, the imperfections are what make anything hand-made—personalised—all the more precious.

Possibly the most complex one I have built was a massive Fitness First–inspired dreaMCatcher that took nine hours to create after sourcing all the required resources. The hoop and web were weaved on a bicycle wheel that was then decorated with three kilograms of training-themed charms: skipping rope, free weights, mini boxing gloves, tiny runners, metal chains, weight clips and 13 metres of rope, in the colour of the Fitness First brand.

All have been made with care and freely gifted to people in my circle or as a giveaway to inspire motivation and action towards personal goals. Some have been exceptionally personal, channelling a deep love and respect for the intended recipient. All, as far as I'm aware, have been joyfully received.

The value of something hand-made, real effort, taps into emotions of feeling loved and appreciated. It's easy to buy a gift, even if we do struggle at times thinking what may be a suitable present to give. To bequest something hand-made with personal effort shows appreciation of a different kind altogether. We all know it.

To highlight this I have for many years used a simple relatable example to attest to the perceived value of personalisation. Holding up a sheet of paper or showing a slide on screen I ask an audience:

'Who has a picture like this?'

The image is of a child's drawing: an interpretation of the family home on a sunny day.

'How many of you (reading this even) have such a picture on your fridge, office desk or hanging on the walls?'

'And who drew that picture for you?'

Usually the answers are the kids, nieces or nephews, grandchildren, godchildren or friends' kids. It doesn't matter how badass or grumpy you are, I've found even the most hardened of souls feel a spark of joy as two tiny hands pass over an artwork they've expended energy uncomfortably creating while sprawled across the floor. (Even if some of the crayons and paints have stained the carpets in the process.)

'For you,' they cutely mumble, giggling or smiling, then running away after gifting you the masterpiece.

You love it because of who drew it and what it represents. Personalised or hand-made effort is pure love.

On a recent nationwide tour across Australia I ran this activity with Optus teams.

On asking a show of hands in Perth for who had such a picture, about one-third of the audience's hands went up: which is a pretty typical response.

I honed in on a gentleman down the back row.

'And who did that picture for you, sir?'

The young gent shrugged and wryly smiled as he responded, 'I don't actually know'.

I was confused. Everyone was laughing, looking at him with puzzlement and so he explained.

'I recently moved into a new place. The picture was already stuck on the fridge. I kind of liked it so I just left it there.'

It attests to the powerful energy of such efforts. That even a random stranger's kids, leaving a house-warming gift for the new tenant, might provoke feelings of positive emotion.

It can be the simple things like messaging someone, or better still phoning, on their birthday or a special occasion of any kind. It's a surprising delight that someone may remember your favourite colour, coffee preference or a multitude of idiosyncrasies, quirky preferences or little-known hobbies. And when was the last time you received a hand-written love letter? Okay, to be clear, from someone you know and like, not the personalisation that comes from inappropriately crossing intimacy lines in the style of a stalker.

The digital age makes many aspects of personalisation easier. Guests checking into hotels are welcomed by name on the television screen as they enter the room. Far more memorable may be when the hotel goes to the extra effort of taking colourful whiteboard markers and creatively scribbling funkier salutation messages on the mirrors.

Any kind of personalisation and handmade effort explodes the warm and fuzzy feel-good factor of value. And to ramp it up another notch, making a lasting impression that makes people go 'wow' is priceless.

4. Leaps in creative faith: innovation

You might have heard of John Lasseter. If you haven't, you'll certainly know—no doubt love—characters created from his influence and vision.

Back in 1975 he was a fresh-faced programmer with an eye on the potential of computer animation. He even did a stint at Disney. At that time though, unless new methods of graphics and animation could be made faster or cheaper they were unlikely to inspire investment. The ideas and formulas John was passionate about went against the grain in this regard. So John was fired.

As John Lasseter was to the world of animated storytelling, so Ed Catmull was to the world of computer graphics and computer science. Ed was integral in founding many tools and systems in the invention of 3D graphics, as we know them. (For the geeks among us: Z-buffer, texture mapping and subdivision surfaces.)

John and Ed teamed up. They shared a common vision in wanting to be the first to produce a full-length animated feature film completely from computer animation. You may be thinking today, 'So what? That's no big deal' but this was 1983 and the goal proved to be quite some time away.

Ed invited John to join his division working at Lucasfilm: founded by George Lucas and home of *Star Wars*. Their time in the Lucasfilm environment allowed space for experimentation. They produced the first completely computer-generated scene in a blockbuster movie (*Star Trek: Wrath of Khan*) and the first completely computer-generated character (Young Sherlock Holmes). It was also where they began creating animated short films. *The Adventures of Andre and Wally B* was the first in what later became a kind of tradition.

Playing in the space of innovating computer-generated animation they found that the ideal tools of the trade they required simply didn't exist. So they had to invent hardware and software programs. The Pixar Image Computer is the first mention of the duo-syllabic name the world associates as cool: PIXAR was born, just not in the form we now know it.

George Lucas had zero interest in making full-length feature animations. The bulk of his films were to remain flesh and blood actors. Luke Skywalker, Chewbacca and Han Solo were fine zipping around computer-generated universes but they weren't destined as cartoons in their search for the force. There weren't so many aligned visionaries willing to take a leap of faith around in the real world either. But one did show up.

Steve Jobs, after being fired from his own passion project and baby—Apple—in 1985 founded his next company, ironically called 'Next'. Jobs decided to buy the Graphics Group (PIXAR's name at the time) from George Lucas for $5 million dollars. It was considered a decent sum in the day. But then, when you read about Jobs's hands-on involvement (high dominant preference) and direction on Apple Inc. projects he bled far more tangible finances in the pursuit of perfecting a single button or feature on many of his own creations.

The reason PIXAR appealed to Jobs may also be another similarity. Lasseter and Catmull's vision was simply too far ahead of market readiness. Even with Steve Jobs's backing and involvement the business faced bankruptcy multiple times. For a period of more than 10 years PIXAR was essentially a computer hardware and software company, not the animation studio we think of. While John Lasseter continued creatively beavering away spending time and money on groundbreaking animation, the business managed to stay afloat selling or leasing packages including proprietary ones such as 'Renderman'. Steve Jobs came close to selling, reportedly losing a million dollars a year for five years. But as is often the case with inspiring stories, the darkest hour was right before the dawn.

One of their early short films was a story about an adjustable desktop lamp and its offspring entitled *Luxo Jr.* It went on to be the first CGI film ever nominated for an Academy Award, Best Animated Short Film, in 1986.

During his experimentation with animated short films, Lasseter latched onto an idea about toys escaping from a baby. This became the basis of the storyboard behind *Toy Story*. Disney was interested and opted to be back in the mix. But after a year of preparation, the production was halted and shut down. Disney either wasn't convinced of the direction John was taking or plain didn't like it.

Disney's backing once again turning cold may well have spelled the end. But John and the team at PIXAR kept true to their own vision. They focused on making *Toy Story* the way they knew they wanted to. While the movie took five years in total to make, in the end Disney liked it. It was the highest grossing movie in 1995: estimated at taking over $190 million domestically in the United States and over $360 million worldwide.

It turns out that the majority of profit in the business of computer animation is, surprise surprise, not from the movie itself but rather the highly profitable, sought-after merchandise and products associated with the characters we have come to love.

PIXAR went on to be the biggest IPO listed in 1995, raising over $130 million.

It renegotiated contracts with Disney as equal partners on all fronts. Its second film, *A Bug's Life*, released in 1998, was to become the most successful film of its year and continued to set a trend.

There are many things we can take from their journey. To simplify this, or their philosophies, and say 'be innovative like PIXAR' would exclude both the myriad and depth of lessons. It's the detail in overcoming a broad selection of challenges, achieving specific period milestones, birthing systems or technologies and even combatting staid practices or culture that reveals the value of creativity and innovation.

Typically in Hollywood, movies are decided upon through a top-down mentality. The bosses select what gets made. In PIXAR everybody has a chance to pitch ideas.

John Lasseter has said of ideas, 'We all hold hands, jump and figure out the parachute'. Meaning they'll collectively invent, then create whatever is needed given it's been a part of their DNA from the very beginning. The democratically popular ideas animators passionately get behind allow the storytelling to get into their heart, souls and brains. The egalitarian efforts in turn travel down their arms and out of their hands to manifest into the world so that we can be introduced to new characters we're delighted to add to toy and movie collections gathering on the shelf.

PIXAR operates in a purpose-built open space. This anti-establishment environment ensures people aren't siloed. They believe it's in the walking, talking, eating, drinking and playing together that a bubbling laboratory of animation, experimentation, innovation and valuable collaboration is born.

Possibly one of the most powerful lessons is best said—as a tribute to those early ties with Lucasfilm—in the anastrophe speech style of the Star Wars character Yoda: 'For innovation value to flourish, have patience young padawan. Rust art you must not!

The total development time, if you consider ideas formed and storyboarding, may take four to six years. The actual production time is closer to one-and-a-half to two years. Yet the outputs must be a standard Pixar and Disney will be happy with so the bottom line is it will take however long it takes.

One of their secret ingredients is the ability to invent relatable characters amid important themes and inspiring messages. And they do it without telling, lecturing or preaching. They understand well the secret of storytelling is that people will make up their own minds.

Their films are as much for adults as kids. Woody's fear of being replaced by the new, shiny toy Buzz Lightyear reflects people's fears towards change, acceptance and kindness.

A *Bugs Life*, inspired by the Aesop's fable *The Ant and the Grasshopper*, shares how even a crew of misfits, apparent outsiders, can overcome challenges of the downtrodden or stand up to overzealous advances of greed.

Nemo the clown fish teaches much about dealing with and overcoming fears. His father Marlin gives insight into the art of letting go: you can't control every external force. Personally I love the forgetful Dory. When training presentation skills I adapt her philosophy of 'just keep swimming' for the benefit of presenters who have a tendency to get stuck trying to remember an exact fact or word. Just keep going! Nobody except you knew what you were going to say anyway.

Wall-E relates to current global topics of over-consumption, the state of our planet and over-reliance on technology—with human beings becoming overweight, somewhat dim and lazy. It's potentially their one film that carries the exceptionally relevant current messages of human connection and protecting the environment.

My personal favourite though has to be the university and world of *Monsters, Inc.* Sulley, the best scarer that ever is, was or will be, ultimately learns that a child's laughter is 10 times more powerful than a child's screams. If that's not love over fear personified—monstafied even—then I don't know what is. I'm proud to say I have several movies, the short films collection and my own cuddly Sulley mascot. You're welcome, PIXAR, for my contribution to your $14 billion pot.

So, in true Aesop's Fables style, the moral of the PIXAR story is this...

• All creativity is valuable.

• Not all creativity is innovation or disruptive. (A term devalued by overuse!)

- Innovation only comes from creative experimentation.

- Innovation opens doors to potentially massive tangible value windfalls.

At one point people looked at John's animation team and their efforts were considered a waste of resources, dollars and time. Their approach bolsters the power in combined elements of value with storytelling, sensory engagement and creativity pursued with passion and personal value compounding to fruition over time. They've built up equity and popularity in an iconic brand while simultaneously, smartly so, procuring a solid partnership with Disney alleviating the risks associated with innovating animated stories that may take years and hundreds of millions of dollars to produce. As of 2019 PIXAR has released 21 full-length features estimated at $14 billion plus in worldwide gross revenues. And they've generated way more than that globally in the feel-good factor.

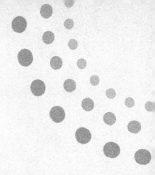

Emotional value
Tools, tips and self-reflEQtion

The most important person in your world is you. If you're not okay, not feeling the best version of yourself, it's unlikely you'll radiate as a light for others. The other person is the most important person in their world for exactly the same reason.

This short list aims to provoke opening a treasure trove of emotional value. But don't feel compelled to follow only these. Invent your own and get creative! These aren't designed as the only tools with which to tap and expand emotional states or awareness.

Killing outdated personal stories

What tales or beliefs do you keep telling yourself that don't make you feel so great? Get off the subject! Acknowledge where they have come from, sure, then soften them and focus on a different story. Be, do or go after the things in life that make you feel good. In that order! Start by being happy. You don't need to have anything to feel the value of life.

Share better stories with others

Should you wish to become a better storyteller (or try to resolve a conflict or perhaps position an initiative or product) find creative metaphors that are easy to relate to and have better relevance for the target individual or audience. Then work on refining storytelling and presentation skills. I've got a whole program—'ORATOR'—on this subject but consider such things as:

- *voice influences*: animation, enunciation, description, volume or silence

- *body language influences*: breath, posture, eye contact, nervous habits

- *design influences*: structure, edit, purpose, creativity, personal values

- *in delivery*: energy, engagement, nobody knew what you were going to say.

Explore your senses

Set up experiences forcing you to leverage your inherent senses to full capacity! Invite friends along for the ride. Food tastings, music genres or themed nights, attempt to identify objects while blindfolded, go to day spas! There's a stack of board games you can play. Look for ways to heighten your awesome sensory awareness.

Get off devices and have tech-free time or days

A part of the reason our senses are numbed is due to the level of noise around us and our addiction to technology. Elect a completely free day/weekend where technology will be for emergencies only. Detox from social media and the likes. Put attention back on your real world. When you're out with friends focus on feeling, not photographing, the whole experience. Create more memories and collect more mental pictures than photos.

Find your 'Rosebud' and play with a creative hobby

You're a creative being even if you don't feel it. Creativity is not about perfection. Choose something you can do to get down and dirty with your hands. Put time aside for drawing, painting, handcrafts, cooking, dancing, learning an instrument or dabbling with mechanics: anything that invests time building or creating something from a blank canvas.

Create a handmade gift

Show others how important they are by spending a little of your precious time on a creation for an individual, group or specific scenario. Perhaps there are people in your world you don't say 'thank you' to quite frequently enough. Who are the two, three, four or five people you can surprise with a treat for a special occasion or just because you can? Whoever or whatever springs to mind, secretly work on a handmade gift for a pleasant surprise. Remember any imperfections are part of the beauty of the gift.

Delight your customers

Spend some time thinking how to combine creativity and personalisation, then take some of those ideas to fruition to make your friends or customers go 'wow'! Do this with your team or business and build a collaborative mastermind playbook for personalisation or experience. Don't just think about a 'product'; think about the whole experience to wrap around it. The software company Qualtrics adds value by putting a larger focus on experience (which is emotional). It has a four-part experience made up of product, brand, customer, employee.

4

Service value

Enrich other people's lives

The great Muhammad Ali said, 'Service to others is the rent you pay for your room here on earth'.

A friend of mine, Natalie, was in Japan on a business trip in 2003. She decided to procure a unique personalised gift for me: kanji. She thought logographic symbols representing primary words epitomising the nature of my character would be a pleasant surprise. Plus it might match other personal décor in my home, a modest combination of quirky objets d'art symbolic of my life and travels.

She figured finding bespoke providers of kanji in Japan would prove straightforward. But apparently not. I'll share my memory of the story of her experience. Though some of the finer details of flashbacks may be a little flawed, the gist and feeling are fact.

After unsuccessfully finding any shop or even street artist who offered the service, Natalie turned to plan B. Hotel receptions are a handy go-to for local knowledge the world over. And even if they're not armed with immediate intelligence they have the advantage of speedy internet at their fingertips and fewer barriers like language.

The lady at reception pointed out that while kanji is traditional—found everywhere from luminous signs to pamphlets—it's not a typical business people aspire to. Earning a living scribing symbols for visitors may be entrepreneurial but it is even less common than street art. Or certainly it was at the time.

The variety of phonebooks, business guides and Japanese equivalents of advertising directories grabbed from behind the reception booth, which doubled as an encyclopaedic counter, delivered no bites. Reinforcements were called in: she asked her more senior colleague.

They spent some time spitballing ideas. There was scratching of heads, moments of puzzled silence and occasional fits of giggles. You know, ridiculous ideas thrown into the fray to break stagnant dead ends to get things moving, being laughed off and shot down. It was time for the big guns. The concierge.

An experienced concierge is worth their weight in gold when it comes to local knowledge and getting stuff done, especially when the requests are somewhat off the beaten path of mainstream tourist enquiries. They've established a little black book of often-bizarre contacts, either front of mind or tucked in the pocket ready to go. If, for example, you found yourself in Russia and for some strange reason wanted to get your hands on a bright souvenir Contiki staff shirt from the 1990s or dodgy CDs with titles misspelt, I know a contact in Tver who'll be able to help. Yet on this occasion, even after street contacts were pressed and favours were called in, still she had no luck.

So it came to pass that the regional hotel manager was called in. Being in charge of multiple concierges and locations, perhaps casting a wider net would catch the fish.

We've now got two duty reception clerks, a concierge, a duty manager (who'd curiously joined in) and a regional manager working the case.

If that's not impressive enough, what comes next surely is, both in relation to service and quality leadership.

After listening to and discussing intently, in Japanese, the pickle at hand, along with the string of failed avenues ventured, this senior figure paused for a moment. He then offered a nougat of pay dirt, delivered directly in English for my friend to understand, that might overcome the dilemma:

'I believe one of the staff who works part time in our kitchen practises calligraphy in her art studies. I think she may also be working today. Let's ask.'

It turns out he was right. The junior kitchen hand working in service in the restaurant was undertaking courses studying art and design. She had a passion for calligraphy. She was on duty and she joined the rest of the gang. As the request was described, her nodding head indicated a solution had indeed been found. It turns out she also had the required materials. The high-quality rice papers and artistic pens were in her locker. The senior leader gave her permission to take further time from her duties to help Natalie secure the bespoke kanji she sought.

By this stage all the fuss had garnered the interest of other guests. Some thought what a wonderful gift idea this was. They too were then keen to get some kanji done. However, the kindness and permission given for the time of the kitchen hand extended only to Natalie in this instance.

If you know about Japanese traditions like the tea ceremony, you know attention to detail means such things may take up to four hours. So imagine the concentration and dedicated effort exhibited by the student to complete this over a period of some 45 minutes. Her attention to detail brought four bespoke kanji to life.

Three of them, for three specific words, were completed on the same set of beautifully, slightly speckled A4 paper. These are now a wonderful feature framed in my home. The fourth, a variation in kanji for one of the words, was completed on a separate quality sheet. I occasionally roll it out at talks to share as an anecdotal lesson for several themes.

One of the questions I'm commonly asked is, 'Which words do the kanji represent?' My answer here is, 'You may find out at some of my live events'. It's nice at times to be left wanting a little more, plus, in addition to being playful, I wonder whether Natalie would nominate the same traits? They may remain a core part of my character, yet layers of life experiences and personal value have developed over the years since, possibly making others more relevant to the man I am now.

Imagine the words to be your own. What might they be? Whatever the words, having them skilfully crafted and capturing the essence of one person's soul as seen through the eyes of another then generously gifted as a surprise is a treasured souvenir aligned with another element of value.

The thing I love most about the entire unfolding of this event is that neither the hotel nor the girl would accept any kind of payment for their service. They refused all insistence as the fine finished products were ceremoniously handed over. Natalie was visiting for a conference and wasn't even a guest staying in this hotel and they knew that. Yet none were deterred from helping find a solution. It's a reason I've continued to spruik or recommend the Yokohama Royal Park Hotel.

I'm frequently reminded, transfixed at times when staring at the kanji on my walls out of interest—not boredom—of Muhammad Ali's quote at the beginning of this chapter and his attitude towards service to others. The world would be a lonely place if we were stuck here all alone. Yet often we forget that.

Chefs you never meet working in kitchens your eyes never see feed you sustenance on trips for both business and pleasure. The watch on your wrist, the craftsmanship of some stranger perhaps as far away as Switzerland, allows you to remain punctual.

Even the drivers of delayed public transport are souls doing the best they can to get you to your destination safely, even if sometimes a little late.

Many people will invest their precious time to write complaints or voice concerns over annoyances, disapproval or letdowns. Fewer will go out of their way to proactively invest equal or greater amounts of time with the same diligence to pay homage or show gratitude.

After working for so many years in travel, I can promise the service staff who some people feel compelled to yell abuse at have no desire either to be held up. That's why I'll happily be the annoying guy hollering 'thank you' from halfway down the crowded bus.

Yes, I do know too, there are some who work in fields of service who forget the nature of their roles. There are plenty of curmudgeons, both young and old, in a fast-paced consumerist world driven all too frequently by selfish, blinkered motivation. People may lose patience too quickly, react too harshly or judge unilaterally without thought. Perhaps we can remind them that gratitude and quality service may be tools to snap them from the grips of their grumpiness.

Maybe we can take a lesson from that student in Yokohama. I've found that many descriptions of what people perceive as most valuable fall into categories where we apply ourselves in very specific ways with dedicated effort. So like a pen to rice paper (or fingers to a keyboard in this digital era) consider the following four dichotomies, which constitute the essence of service value. Doing so may ensure the payments we make as rent are valuable attitudes and behaviours to the world.

Service value in a nutshell

The four dichotomies are questions to ask ourselves as a check-in to ensure we're paying our rent in service:

1. Problem–Solution
2. Possibilities–Consequences
3. Self–Others
4. The environment: to wreck or nurture

1. Problem–Solution

When people hear that my journey in human development began in travel, training frontline leaders for Contiki Holidays, I often hear comments along the lines of:

- 'That's cool! You were on holiday all the time then!'
- 'What a lifestyle—I wish mine was like that.'
- 'You must have had a ball.'

On occasion, rigid-thinking corporate types have pondered:

- 'So how does that translate to leadership?'
- 'That sounds fun, but what practical operational skills does that arm you with?'
- 'Leading tour groups is not like business though, is it?'

Since those Contiki days, I've worked for more than two decades as an experienced practitioner in the field of training, learning and development. I've assisted global projects and a multitude of blue-chip businesses: hands-on involvement of establishment frameworks and capabilities in leadership, sales, operations, culture and much more, often from a standing start. I can unequivocally say I'm yet to face a single body of work with anywhere near the complexities or problem-solving skills required as those demanded frontline on tours, no matter your perception of an environment like Contiki.

The brand has built an amazing reputation—good and bad, but mostly good—over the course of six decades. Founder John Anderson was also on the speaking circuit for many years, sharing fascinating stories of how this iconic touring company was founded.

Wishing to travel around Europe for free, Anderson positioned himself as a tour guide in spite of having no experience or credibility to speak of. He interviewed enough potential passengers to fill a mini bus. Having calculated the approximate total cost, he divided the required budget by the number of passengers, ensuring his own seat as organiser was free. Then he did it all again with two mini buses. The early ethos was more along the lines of 'just follow me, even if I'm lost too' rather than worrying too much about getting lost. The depth of knowledge and intricacies of logistics required for the polished product of Contiki would come years later.

Highly respected former long-serving 'captain' of Contiki, DDH (David) Hosking (a great man!) summed up the responsibility of being a tour operator: touring has to be a lot of fun, but it has to be done with diligence, compliance, a healthy dose of common sense and with both the safety and respect of all passengers in mind.

He'd bring these principles to life leveraging a single typical passenger persona (fact or fiction is still to be determined). 'Meet Mary Wells from Wagga Wagga. She's spent the past two years of her life working hard, simultaneously saving money and putting it aside as a travel kitty. She might persist with this habit for two years in order to save the approximately $20k required for her big overseas adventure. And along with Mary you're going to have 49 other people just like her. So that's a million dollars invested, sitting behind you on a coach, excitedly ready for the experience of a lifetime. No pressure. Just don't f*ck up. And if you do, fix it!'

In other words, for every aspect of any role—say, for example, that of a trainee Contiki tour leader—consider that if it's not done properly, problems will arise. If logistics are not dealt with or set up appropriately, then the tour will come unstuck. If quality presentations are not delivered, or if you get lost due to a lack of planning, the customer experience will deteriorate—potentially along with the group dynamics. Solutions have to be pre-empted or delivered as needed.

Let's use 'James' as an example. He may have grown up on a farm or in a remote location in Australia. Perhaps even Wagga Wagga.

James held a desire, like John Anderson, to have a big overseas adventure and to do it for free or even be paid in the process. So James applied to be a Contiki tour leader.

Successfully navigating the group interviews showcasing his capabilities meant progression to the second stage amid a harsh selection process.

The second interview was intense and at times provocatively personal. It was one way to weed out talent that lacked the fundamental skills or initiative required, or that may be difficult to mould in order to handle the role.

James, now selected as a potential trainee for his 'easy' dream job, has about eight weeks to participate in and survive a live training tour—London to Istanbul and back to London—to show he's up for the task at hand. If he isn't, his training manager can eject him from his seat anywhere along the way and the $500 bond he's put up as part of the condition for his place, will be forfeited.

As part of the training, James is expected to absorb a long list of information, including:

- learning every route and turn the coach must take and making sure you know what's required for tolls, fuel stops, toilet drops and legal parking every step of the way

- gaining intimate knowledge about every country and being prepared to deliver multiple talks on them without reading from notes

- learning about the history of every country, city or major site of interest you pass and making sure you bring each city to life with depth of stories and facts—all from memory

- finding out details about every major monument, museum and place of interest: where are they, what time they open or close and how much they cost

- knowing the cost of a cup of coffee, beer or wine—hell, even a Mars bar—in every location, as well as the cost of using public toilets...

You get the gist. Effectively, even if James makes it, he will be paid an abysmal amount to handle everyone else's problems and create solutions where needed.

The single most valuable lesson to learn on a training tour is the one I'll call 'what if'. What if...

- passports or tour funds get lost or stolen?

- your entire coach gets stolen in the Eastern Bloc or Russia?

- you lose passengers in a city or country?

- the coach catches fire in one of the longest road tunnels in Europe?

- passengers are arrested or detained by police?

- three passengers are run over by the same car in Venice: a city of water!

- your coach is involved in a minor accident, rolling over or significantly crashing?

- 17 passengers, along with a driver and three local guides, perish in a heart-breaking canyoning catastrophe?

Arming trainees for these and a million other scenarios you wish never to happen or can't even fathom was perhaps the single most important lesson to instil.

The fiction of tour brochures, which build the illusion of this 'easy dream job', is the reason that some people then find it hard to connect relevance to leadership skills, operational efficiencies, selling or even critical problem solving.

In every tour brochure the sun is shining, there's never any scaffolding, the queues waiting in line aren't horrendous and everybody is smiling. It's like the fictional town where Truman Burbank lives, where nothing goes wrong and everything is friendly—lattés, cocktails and bliss. The reality can, of course, be eye-opening, testing, stressful and quite different.

Even for a company like Contiki (which specialises in 18–35-year-old tourists) the people who love the metrics of tangible value—such as statisticians—will attest that the law of probability doesn't work in your favour. When your business transports 50000 passengers or so each year, the law of average dictates, sadly, you're going to have more than your fair share of daily problems or tragedies.

For me as a rep, leader and training manager, the Contiki environment cemented the importance of this first self-reflective dichotomy of service value.

Flip the switch

In anything you do, if you don't have your act together and aren't diligent with your efforts you'll likely be either a part or primary reason for problems that f*ck up anything, not just million-dollar experiences of a lifetime.

Anyone can throw their hands up in despair or holler and complain how bad everything is. Kids can berate adults for screwing up the world. It's noble to be passionate about highlighting problems or rallying support for worthy causes. But anyone—everyone—can do that. Being of service means bringing depth of wisdom, ideas and solutions instead of just fighting or rebelling against the things we disapprove of.

The essence of Einstein's thinking captures well the importance of comprehension to both sides of the equation:

> We cannot solve our problems with the same thinking we used when we created them…If I had an hour to solve a problem I'd spend 55 minutes thinking about the problem and 5 minutes thinking about solutions.

Yes, we need to understand any problem in detail in order to identify the most valuable solution. But at some point we must flip the switch in our brain from problem analysis to solution thinking. It's literally a different part of your brain, with neurons and connections firing up that will tap the required precious insights and ideas.

Often people remain stuck in the problem. They may not realise the nature of their internal ramblings isn't helping—those silent downloads where we just can't for the life of us stop looking at the problem even when we think we've moved on. When I'm:

- talking about the problem, I'm looking at the problem
- describing causes for the problem, I'm still looking at the problem
- explaining what hasn't worked, I'm still looking at the problem
- explaining that others have similar challenges, I'm still looking at the problem.

All is fine when used for conscious problem analysis. It's when those conversations become shared repeatedly as ongoing status updates to tell 10, 20 or 100 people the same drama that we're stuck in the emotion of the problem itself. Asking for input from people you know have something credible to offer is more of a solution tact. When:

- asking what we've not yet tried, I'm searching for solutions

- asking how others overcome similar challenges, I'm solution searching

- free-thinking creative, innovative ideas, I'm inviting doors to solutions

- open-mindedly inviting suggestions from others, I'm solution thinking.

Service value, personally or professionally, is asking this first self-reflective puzzling question more frequently: *Is what I'm doing creating or adding to problems or solutions?* Service value is identifying, then analysing, existing headaches or potential threats. Service value is also having a willingness and capability to find, in collaboration if need be, appropriate solutions. Service value is about being pre-emptive in our thinking: to elucidate solutions before the problem is even a problem.

2. Possibilities–Consequences

Paris night tour departing Palais de Chaillot, Trocadéro

As we crawl slowly along Avenue Kléber I have two choices of music to pick from. What music should I play for the ambiance?

Shall we go Dick Dale's *Misirlou*? You know, the pumping guitar riff made famous by the opening titles in the movie *Pulp Fiction*. Or shall we go classical? 'In the Hall of the Mountain King' from the *Peer Gynt Suite* by Edvard Grieg?

The challenge with Grieg is the timing. It's a best guess when creeping along Avenue Kléber as to when to hit <play>. It takes precisely 1 minute 45 seconds of gradual escalation in foot tapping rhythm before morphing into the frenzied, lofty, iconic culmination. If it drops at just the right time it will maximise the effect when we hoon hair rousingly onto the roundabout that lies ahead. While with *Misirlou* I just hit <play> and the effect on excitement is immediate.

Either soundtrack will elevate the atmosphere. It's the small touches such as this that compound to create that million-dollar experience. The impending roundabout in question is the one circling the magnificent Arc de Triomphe.

Once amid the fray—*Misirlou* or *Mountain King*—it's a hell of a buzz for first-time riders. After circling the arch a couple of times, usually amid a combination of cheering, laughter and screams, it's time to fade the music and let those storytelling skills kick in.

Napoleon's victory arch

The Arc de Triomphe is one of the largest triumphal arches in the world, standing 50 metres high and 45 metres wide. It's also one of the most celebrated and visited sites by tourists flocking to the city of lights.

Reliefs carved at the base of the four sturdy pillars represent battle scenes and victories from the Napoleonic era. One of them is the 'Departure of the Volunteers of 1792', which depicts the departure of a French revolutionary army, being led into battle by a sword-carrying warrior representing France. Most people more commonly know the relief under another name, that of the French national anthem *La Marseillaise*.

Other reliefs include trophies and friezes representing soldiers going into battle. On the inside walls of the monument are names of significant figures during the Napoleonic wars, including over 550 generals. If the commanders have their name underlined it means they died in battle. Any remaining spare space on the memorial is dedicated to slightly less important, though no less trivial, victories or recognition.

Paris is ripe, or perhaps rife depending how you look at it, with spectacular yet smug self-congratulatory trophies of so many of Napoleon Bonaparte's achievements. He was an interesting if somewhat egotistical character: small in stature yet large in presence.

Born in Corsica in 1769, Napoleon rose rapidly through the military ranks to prominence after the French Revolution, becoming a general at the age of 24.

By 1799 he was the First Consul of the Republic. Being citizen number one amid the centralised republic still wasn't quite cutting the French mustard as a suitably splendid salutation for his business card. So in 1804 he changed it to 'Emperor of France'.

For all his smarts, it was Napoleon's dream of extending his empire that was to be his downfall. It was 1812 when Napoleon's Grande Armée—at over 650000 strong potentially the largest gathered in history—crossed the Neman River. The plan in Napoleon's brain was to rapidly defeat and conquer the Russians. The pride of the Cossacks led them to equally cunning tactics. They drew the French forces, and Napoleon's ego, further into the vastness of their empire scorching the earth with each retreat.

While the French claimed another victory with a static battle at Borodino, west of Moscow, the French casualties numbered tens of thousands. The harsh Russian winter kicked in and the demoralised, declining numbers were forced to retreat. By the time the Grande Armée exited Russian soil close to 400000 had perished in battle or due to the severe conditions.

Napoleon was exiled to Elba, off the coast of Tuscany, but he managed to escape for a little more than 100 days as a final 'hurrah' (or perhaps he was curious to see how the ongoing construction on the Arc de Triomphe was going). Austria, Russia, Prussia and Britain joined forces fighting Napoleon's French all stars. This single campaign was to be a winner-takes-all game of two halves. It was close! The British army alliance, under command of the Duke of Wellington, held ground until the Prussians, held up in a simultaneous battle, arrived as late substitutes to essentially save the day. 18 June 1815 was Napoleon's red card.

That final battlefield name became synonymous as a metaphor for anyone taking action where consequences haven't been fully thought through: everyone has their Waterloo.

He might have left his hopes in France but his hubris surely followed Napoleon to the location of his final exile: the bleak, remote, volcanic island of St Helena, 1900 kilometres from the nearest landmass off the west coast of Africa. He asked his jail keepers to acknowledge him by his self-proclaimed title as Emperor of France. They refused. He bickered over conditions of his prison home on St Helena until he finally persuaded the British Governor to sponsor an upgrade to Longwood House, which was also a far cry from the comforts and splendour of his beloved former residence, Fontainebleau Palace. All the while he might have been wondering if his Arc de Triomphe was finished yet. It wasn't. He died in 1821 waiting on modest renovations to his prison home to be finished.

Napoleon's final resting place at Les Invalides in Paris contains a purpose-built, gold-domed chapel holding his tomb. His captors may not have respected his wishes but in the end Napoleon had the last guffaw. He achieved his dying wish: to be buried on the banks of the Seine close to the people of France he loved, though not until 1940 as he was first buried on Saint Helena Island.

I'm sure beneath it all, those six long years on that remote island is where Napoleon finally had plenty of opportunity to feel the full impact of his choices and to reflect on many 'what ifs'. The apparently uninviting, rodent-infested, cold abode he found himself holed up in for his final days would have reminded him of the hardships of that catastrophic Russian winter. Where it all turned to custard and went horribly wrong.

Had Napoleon paused to understand the intensity of personal value magnified by the layers of his own character (dominant style preference, with a motivation that was individualistic and a strong ego) perhaps the story may have turned out differently. If only he'd been more adept at pausing to take stock or pondered advice from critical advisors for longer, he might have marvelled with his own eyes his wondrous Arc de Triomphe instead of being towed lifeless beneath it.

His biggest regret may lie in his lack of skill in leveraging one of the strongest traits of his very own personal symbol and motif—the eagle. I like to think he might have stumbled on some enlightenment, thinking back to his aspirations when first glancing east. He was short sighted by only considering the possibility side of the equation. He misinterpreted the Russian psyche and wasn't willing to fathom the dire consequences of a decimated army. He only envisaged the possibility that the backyard Cossack farm mouse would surely be easy prey for his eagle.

History continually teaches consequences

There are many events and characters worthy of discussion as cautionary tales. By looking back into our collective past we may learn great lessons that reflect the critical importance of realising full consideration to both aspects of this specific dichotomy, possibilities and consequences: two peas in a pod in every daily choice.

So it's timely to now take a moment and expand a little on the man who helped turn the tide of that Great Depression we spoke of in the history of money. Franklin D Roosevelt (FDR) had a couple of things in common with Napoleon.

Like Napoleon, he was a man of far-reaching ambition. He had his sights set on a senior office from a young age.

Academics and historians alike often agree the single major setback in FDR's life, being crippled by polio in adulthood, potentially armed him with a fuller set of skills. He was forced, or learned, to sculpt the traits that are his enduring legacy: curious, resilient and armed with a healthy dose of temperance, calmness and empathy.

FDR leveraged the first of what was to become known as his 'fireside chats' via radio broadcast in his first presidential term, which began in 1933. The 15-minute broadcast and strategy settled hearts and minds amid the slump of the Great Depression.

During his fireside chats in World War II FDR encouraged people to buy world maps and have them at hand for each occasion. He'd then systematically walk listeners through simplified strategies and overviews of what was really happening in various locations of the global conflict. This highlights again the power of banking emotional value via instruments of storytelling and engaging people's senses. Invested, they would follow along visually and kinaesthetically to the calming auditory presidential commentary.

When asked and encouraged by aides to conduct these fireside chats daily, Roosevelt refused. He knew that in doing so they'd lose their potency, authenticity and power. He delivered about 35 in total during his three terms as president.

Damaging possibilities with propaganda

Compare this to Adolf Hitler, who engaged communication tactics, leveraging spin via his devious political machine, the Reich Ministry for Public Enlightenment and Propaganda, headed by Reich Minister Joseph Goebbels. The Nazi regime leveraged big lies deliberately: 'Große Lüge' — big lies — was a term used frequently by Hitler and his henchmen. They believed colossal mistruths would be seen as 'truth' because mass populations wouldn't believe anyone capable of such distortion or lies. Goebbels, a devil after Hitler's own black heart, insisted 'If you tell a lie big enough and keep repeating it, people will eventually come to believe it'.

There's an interesting 'what if' we can ponder with FDR. Amid his curiosity, and against the advice of Fleet Admiral William Leahy, whom he deeply trusted, he sanctioned the Manhattan Project. This ultimately led to the creation of the atomic bomb.

When Roosevelt died on 12 April 1945 they hadn't quite cracked the weapon design.

Harry Truman, FDR's elected vice president, consequently ascended to office by default, the same way Roosevelt had. Thereafter followed a series of consequences.

On 16 July 1945, the outputs of the Manhattan Project were tested in a device known as Trinity, against the advice and protests of scientists.

Truman gave executive orders for the *Enola Gay* and *Bockscar* bombers to conduct unique missions. The consequences of this action are summarised in this history of simple facts:

- Hiroshima: 6 August 1945, 8.14 am. It's a normal, sunny day. *Enola Gay* releases a bomb named 'Little Boy'.

- Hiroshima: 6 August 1945, 8.15 am. Hiroshima is obliterated after the first atomic bomb was dropped. An estimated 70 000 people die within less than a single second. Some, completely incinerated, are vaporised so quickly their actual shadows are eerily preserved etched on concrete.

- Nagasaki: 9 August 1945, 11:01 am. An equally clear day. *Bockscar* releases 'Fat Man'.

- Nagasaki: 9 August 1945, 11:02 am. Nagasaki suffers a similar fate, also being annihilated in less than a minute, with a death toll of 80 000. After Nagasaki, the world started to realise it was dealing with a completely new weapon, with horror stories of immediate after-effects emerging from survivors, such as melted skin and bleeding from all orifices, and others dying slowly of related illnesses.

Truman had been inflexible: he had the bomb and clearly demonstrated his willingness to use it.

What possibilities or consequences were the Japanese thinking about when they surrendered after the second bomb drop, I wonder?

And, even more pertinently, what if Roosevelt hadn't died? Or what if he'd been more transparent with his intentions? Would we have seen atomic actions and consequences?

The lie we're tempted to believe so often is that bombs in World War II were a necessary consequence to save lives. But only a few people had a prime seat to give perspective as to whether such consequences were a necessary evil. A single sentence documented in the pilot's log of the *Enola Gay*, written by co-pilot Robert Lewis, suggests not: *I honestly have the feeling of groping for words to explain this or I might say My God, what have we done?*

Advancement in weaponry or the personal values and morals of leaders in charge of such war machines continually teaches us unfathomable consequences.

The difference between the battles of the Napoleonic era and World War I was huge. At the Battle of Verdun, fought between France and Prussia over the course of a few days, combined casualties were estimated around 11000. At the Battle of Verdun fought during World War I between France and Germany over the course of 303 days, combined casualties were estimated at around 750000.

The step up from World War I to World War II was mammoth again. It's estimated that the total global casualties of World War II was roughly 3 per cent of the total global population.

We may find such history interesting while at the same time thinking 'What can we do to avoid a repeat of this?'

We don't have to be propagandists. The lies we tell, big or small, have consequences on the decisions and actions of others. When we engage in political spin, professionally or personally, or remain truly unbending in any position, there are consequences. When we operate with our egos untethered it may have dire consequences for others.

The fight-or-flight mechanism that makes us run from difficult conversations, or situations of an uncomfortable nature, heads in the sand, doesn't mean the drama or consequences disappear. Doing nothing often has the most severe consequences.

I've deliberately added a little more depth to these historical examples because often the depth is what allows us to feel the consequences. All too frequently we skim the details that allow us to feel the impact.

It's not uncommon to hear people reference hindsight. These tendencies to look backwards with feelings, even if only slight, are frequently described in degrees of regret, remorse or sorrow. Perhaps a lack of patience or empathy, hasty decisions or plain wrongdoing led to disappointing realisations such as:

- 'That's easy to say in hindsight.'
- 'I can see it now looking back.'
- 'I wish I knew back then what I know now.'

Hindsight is defined as wisdom after an event has developed or unfolded.

Wisdom is defined as the quality of experience, knowledge and good judgement, together with the power of using them.

Foresight is defined as an ability to predict what will happen or may be needed in the future.

So hindsight may be foresight when you learn to hit pause on habitual reactions (prior life experiences) and apply wisdom, playing it out to feel longer term possibilities and consequences before they unfold.

The danger looms when we become blind and forget that for every choice we make there is a possibility and a consequence. It's a bona fide scientific fact. Sir Isaac Newton's third law summed it up more than 100 years before Napoleon was born: 'For every action there is an equal and opposite reaction'.

Which is why Napoleon's experiences have also become a synonym for consequences—if you're not careful you too will come face to face with your very own Waterloo.

So, crawling slowly along Avenue Kléber, it's do or die. Which music track to hit <play> on? All this distracted thinking has killed the 1 minute and 45 second lead-in time I had for *Mountain King*. We're going with Pulp Fiction's *Misirlou*!

3. Self–Others

Self-care and selfishness aren't the same thing.

Self-care is putting on your own oxygen mask first, then helping others. Selfishness is putting on your own oxygen mask, then watching others. In extreme cases, it's putting on your own mask, then looking for opportunistic ways to further benefit yourself. Perhaps hoarding masks as spares or capitalising as others struggle.

Balanced Buddhist mantras say, 'May I be at peace. May I be joyful. May I be healthy. May I be happy'.

Or heed the words of American professor Joseph Campbell: 'Follow your bliss!' (Provided that bliss is finding the air of life through your own oxygen mask without impeding the rights of others.)

It's hard to offer service when you're below optimal or if essential elements in life's pyramid of needs are wrecked.

One of my favourite authors, Bryce Courtenay, shared nougats of wisdom relative for both sides of this third dichotomy in his illustrated coffee table book *A Recipe for Dreaming*.

> The helping hands you ... need in life are located at the end of your arms. Put yourself into your own hands. Everybody has two. You can use them to get a hand out, sit on them and do nothing, or ... use them to get a serious grip on yourself.

For every problem there is a solution. All possibilities pursued simultaneously create consequences. The same is true with regard to self-care working in harmonious synergy with consideration of others. ('Self' relates to us and our inner circle. 'Others' relates to the broader community.)

In the documentary *Happy*, Sonja Lyubomirsky (PhD) suggests that three primary pillars impact our overall feeling of inner contentment and happiness:

- *50 per cent* is attributed to a *set point range*, based on our personal genetic makeup

- *10 per cent* is attributed to *circumstances*: income, social status, demographics, age

- *40 per cent* is attributed to *intentional activities*—intentional things we do regularly.

Our circumstances needn't remain static. There are countless real-world Aladdins turning rags into riches who then pass the benefit onto others. Science doesn't suggest all adversity is bad. There can be no joy without knowing a little pain. Some of us are more optimistic: overestimating what might be achieved, especially in a short period of time, or having a preference for daydreaming. Others are perhaps more pessimistic: they may underestimate what could be achieved when we face challenges or tight timeframes. We all have a scaffolding of inner strength made sturdier with external encouragement. We find our way back to whatever that unique generic point may be.

In Bryce Courtenay's *Recipe for Dreaming* he describes how we can face and overcome personal challenges by taking the path less trodden. Doing so invariably means we may face the potential of feeling beaten down, pulled apart and terribly lost. And that's okay because once faced, any challenge becomes what he correctly calls 'experience'. Life experiences are fantastic when, as the 'meaning making machine' you now know you are, you take all of it on board as valuable lessons. What once seemed a rough track becomes a familiar and comfortable, less daunting one. And as an extra benefit the worst things we imagine when taking an unknown road frequently don't unravel or happen.

Realising we can address the combined 60 per cent of generic set point and circumstantial factors, we're left with a sizeable 40 per cent chunk inherent in self-worth through intentional activities. We're generally social creatures with a tendency to compete and collaborate, although when push comes to shove, as the documentary *Happy* shares, more frequently we lean in to cooperate.

Cooperation and collaboration are the simplest forms of philanthropy. The Latin and Greek origins of 'philanthropy' translate literally as meaning 'love of mankind' or 'love of humanity'.

Philanthropy was once primarily associated with the super rich. Wealthy patrons, having experienced or seen the plight of others, might bequeath fortunes, inheritances, scholarships, properties or other resources for the purpose of improving their health and lot. Many organisations born from this love of mankind endure.

Back in 1859 the last battle under the banners and personal command of the monarchs they represented was fought. Napoleon III (Bonaparte's nephew) fought the Sardinian forces under command of the Austrian Emperor Franz Joseph I. The Battle of Solferino was an especially bloody one. There were reports of injured soldiers being turned into fatalities, executed by shootings or bayoneted to death.

A Swiss businessman, Henry Dunant, happened to be in the area and witnessed the aftermath of over 20000 soldiers left wounded or dead. With his innate Swiss precision, he got to organising local civilian communities to provide appropriate care, with Dunant financing the resources required. He wrote about these experiences in *A Memory of Solferino*.

His memoirs incubated an idea of a neutral body dedicated to providing volunteer relief for all those wounded in battle, regardless of whose banner they represented. In 1863, a small, five-person committee, including Dunant, met for the first time, then began turning ideas into action. Dunant ultimately felt he had to resign from his position as a result of bankruptcy and questionable practices. However, the organisation endured.

Decades later, after the dust had settled, Dunant's rightful place as a chief instigator of the respectable humanitarian organisation was recognised and restored. He was honoured with the first ever Nobel Peace Prize. That early committee of five is now global and its logo is among the most distinctive humanitarian bodies on the planet: the International Red Cross.

Planting the seed of philanthropy

Thinking of an example of philanthropy a little closer to home leads me to Andrew Carnegie. The Scottish-American steel magnate was born in Dunfermline, albeit close to 150 years before I moved there as a punchbag. Carnegie spent the better part of his first 65 years amassing his fortune, although always with an eye looking to redirect surplus wealth with benevolence. He's even been quoted as saying 'the man who dies thus rich dies disgraced!' He spent the greater part of his last 20 years redirecting energy and resources to causes aligned with his own values, including the advancement of science and education. There are multiple institutions and trusts that continue to carry his name. It's estimated he founded over 3000 libraries scattered primarily across English-speaking countries including his native Dunfermline. You may have visited one of the many Carnegie Halls around the world to experience musicians or comedians.

More recently, as we already touched on in chapter 2 (Tangible value) Bill and Melinda Gates have leveraged tangible value to compound the service value they provide. The founder of Microsoft turned global philanthropist and humanitarian, Bill, and his wife Melinda, created one of the world's largest private charitable organisations. Launched in 2000, the Bill & Melinda Gates Foundation holds over $50 billion in assets. Like Carnegie, they focus on global issues aligned with their own concerns and values: health and the elimination of poverty. One of the foundation's most valuable assets must surely be the energy and minds of its founders. The docuseries *Inside Bill's Brain*, which highlights the problem-solving skills of geeks, is a great benefit to the world. It's possibly a reason why Warren Buffet, another legendary magnate with an eye on philanthropy, pledged a significant part of his own fortune to help the Bill & Melinda Gates Foundation achieve their goals.

I also find Hamdi Ulukaya, founder of Chobani yoghurt, an inspiring figure. Back in 2005 he turned a former Kraft yard into a healthy Greek yoghurt production plant. Within five years the brand was a leader in the US market and has since expanded globally. A part of its mission since inception has been tithing a percentage of profits into the local communities where company employees live and work. The business also invests in and rewards its people with initiatives such as extended paid leave for new parents and allocation of employee shares, and it hires a significant number of legally resettled immigrants and refugees. Another common thread with Chobani, as with Carnegie, as with the Gates foundation, is the alignment to causes the brand and its leader are passionate about. You might expect the Chobani's feel-good factor to be about improving childhood nutrition through quality foods and total wellness.

There has been a significant shift in the perception blending tangible and service over the past few years. While the bottom line is always a consideration, it can't be at the expense of responsibilities or ethics. The acronym 'CSR' (Corporate/Community Social Responsibility) is now an essential key component to entice employees and customers to bond with brands, ultimately turning them into ambassadors or evangelists. In fact, many people in a consumer mindset describe this clearly. When asked to define value or what's valuable they lean towards products and services that are ethically sound even if more expensive. Adopting CSR (even personally) can be applied via various mechanisms, some traditional and some a little more contemporary:

- tithing, granting stipends or a regular nominated donation
- creation of sponsorships and trusts
- internal employee/department fundraising events
- fundraising matching
- automatic payroll contributions and deductions
- gratuities in the form of purposeful resources or goods
- community style grants
- product- and resource-based support programs
- gifting access to services and specialisations
- supporting local, grassroots communities and schemes
- creating key elements of local community operations
- providing education or health
- donation of property or access to work space
- access to extended influential networks and connections
- paid staff time for hands-on personal effort to support a cause
- the creation of a charity or .org from scratch.

The last couple of examples have perhaps been among the greatest shifts on the philanthropic landscape. Some businesses even allocate a regular amount of time each calendar year for their employees to spend time helping a cause of the employee's own choosing, thus aligned with their own personal value.

A hands-on approach towards philanthropy then is a clear example of where all five values of our Value Model collide: personal value, tangible value, service value, emotional value and relationship value (with the latter being the final value, which we'll get to in the next chapter). We already experienced the power of personal effort engaging the senses. A hands-on approach says 'I care' more than a generous cheque arriving in the post alone.

CSR is among the most sizeable and sustainable ways total value is added to the world. Both corporate and government entities often have wider access to resources, recipients and reach. If they are pioneers, or brave enough, they can invest in better resources or make better choices available for their customers and consumers. Doing so means we are all playing our part in service value in consideration of others. They can also provide and offer the best considered long-term solutions or influence larger adoption through all-important continued education—hopefully shared through powerful stories requiring sensory submersion!

There are entire societies collaboratively experimenting with such concepts in mind. Denmark offers a high standard of living, free college, healthcare and a vast array of benefits for all. Taxes are high, given the funding must come from somewhere, yet so is the service value for the total community. Bhutan, a fledgling economy, prioritises its country's total value not just through traditional, tangible value metrics of GDP (Gross Domestic Product) or GNP (Gross National Product), it also considers and measures GNH: Gross National Happiness.

The path to fulfillment through collaboration is making sure you put your own oxygen mask on, then reach to assist others. Bryce Courtenay again alludes to this in *Recipe for Dreaming* by posing the self-reflective question: *What can we do to add to ourselves so we love ourselves more?* And the best way to answer that question is to do so without the limitations of being time poor or lacking any resources, intelligence or talent. To add value you must make yourself a top priority. By investing in yourself, by feeling good about yourself, you will double down on the reward! The additional self-respect, self-confidence and self-love you feel will radiate into the lives of all others. Everyone benefits more in the end.

Philanthropy, perhaps once perceived as a mechanism reserved for the rich, is easily available at everyone's fingertips. Service value is a participation sport—it is being the best version of yourself in consideration of those possibilities and consequences for others.

4. The environment: to wreck or nurture?

Fifty years ago, 530 million global citizens shared in one of the greatest moments of human achievement as Neil Armstrong placed his foot on the moon. There were two perspectives at the time.

One was an enlivened belief that this event would change humanity forever, opening a future of innovation and excitement, and inspiring generations that they can do anything. Many thought the symbolic nature of this advancement into the heavens—a place we look when searching for answers to the most profound existential questions our life poses—would lead to a change in humankind forever.

The other—the dark side of the moon landing—is summed up best by Gil Scott-Heron in his poem *Whitey on the Moon*, in which he laments that while America is investing all this money into sending a (white) man to space, people are living in abject poverty.

It's a fair point. Should such innovation be a priority given that much of humanity in the one place we all collectively call home has an existential reality including poverty or dire circumstances?

Qualified scientists would explain with far more depth and accuracy the breakthroughs we made as a result of the Apollo missions culminating in achieving the goal of man walking on the moon. The concept of miniaturisation, making things lighter and more compact, has infiltrated every aspect of our lives. Water purification processes have been improved. Even equipment in emergencies, breathing masks and the like, for fire-fighting, have all been made more robust.

Flipping the coin once more, the dark side devil's advocate, there are innovations, perhaps welcomed at the time, that now come under much heat. Polymers (polythene, polyvinyls) and many non-biodegradable substances are headliners these days for all the wrong reasons.

Yet, since this incredible moment of global unity, what have we achieved as humankind? There has been an explosion in innovation and technology, with our world closer together than ever, yet a significant percentage of the planet still lives in poverty. Environmentally, we're choking our planet with pollutants, while manmade evolutions interfere with the natural ecosystems of our planet and threats hang over our heads.

As for the stars, we ceded interest in exploring, more intent in looking at how we can commercialise space. Al Gore spent years endeavouring to get a satellite (DSCOVR) into space with detection equipment aboard that would help provide real, factual data on global climate issues and warnings that could impact everyone—but George W Bush killed the idea.

Such has been our disinterest in exploration, it has now been more than 40 years since a human being last set foot on the moon. The Cassini space probe was one of the most successful space missions of all time, taking some 20 years to reach Saturn and unlock the secrets of the planet, yet most of us are unlikely to have even heard of it.

The early space race was steeped in a genuine wonder for adventure, with a touch of overzealous national pride. There's a renewed interest. Yet the modern-day space race seems more an invitation for the big money and big ego capitalists, with billionaires wanting to have the ultimate joy ride in the experience economy we find ourselves in.

Elon Musk may state his reasoning for wishing to populate Mars as an escape option for humankind. I don't find that particularly inspiring. If we can't collectively sort priorities and get our act together here on Earth, surely we're only likely to repeat the same mistakes on Mars. Migration to the red planet simply spreads any current flaws or human viruses across the universe.

Some countries or corporates are leading the charge by eliminating, reducing or even completely banning unnecessary pollutants and waste such as single-use plastic bags. This is great because, let's be honest, some folks may agree that so much plastic strangling our oceans or used as stuffing for landfill isn't great—yet would they always refuse the item when offered one at the shops?

The travel and tourism industry, one I'm clearly passionate about, is identified as being accountable for as much as 8 per cent of our global carbon emissions impact. Within that, aviation specifically accounts for 2 per cent. Yet when consumers are asked to voluntarily 'neutralise' their footprint, how many people opt in? One per cent. Some airlines perform far greater in this regard and, like companies across all industries, innovate efforts to make required changes. Waste-free flights from Qantas. Jetstar is encouraging passengers to bring their own headphones to reduce the 2.4 million sets of non-recyclable ones handed out in 2018. Air New Zealand announced in 2018 its intention to strip an array of single-use plastic items from its manifests, totalling more than 24 million items per year. This equated to over 50 million operational items in 2019!

Plastic bags, carbon footprints or any one of a multitude of other wasteful woes—take your pick! Corporate- and community-funded or driven initiatives have the ability and power to simplify consumer choices by making the best options available at affordable prices and simultaneously through robust programs of education and training.

If you want some inspiration for a broader list of where and how the world, our collective home, requires a helping hand with service value, look no further than the United Nations' (UN) 'Sustainable Development Goals'. The list of 17 aspirational themes, set for 2030, adopted by UN member states in 2015 is a great reference point. More than half of these address direct human impact on our shared environment—for example:

- clean water and sanitation
- affordable and clean energy
- industry innovation and infrastructure
- sustainable cities and communities
- responsible consumption and production
- climate action
- life below water.

One of these partners, Bill Gates, using his problem-solving mind, shared the surprising initiatives he's backing in his TED Talk, 'Innovating to zero!' They include an unexpected twist on repurposing nuclear waste in the space of affordable and clean global energy. Well worth a watch.

When we talk about the environment we don't need to be pro climate change to realise our choices have consequences. You'd be gutted if someone came around to your home and dumped all their trash. You'd also be out for blood if they hurt anyone or killed your family pet.

When we consider our environment, we can't ignore the threats to the fantastic animals and beasts we share the planet with. Many are so much smarter than us, like those cute baby elephants and dolphins. You'll find lists of creatures whose extinction has been caused by direct human influence: the flightless dodo, the passenger pigeon, the Western black rhinoceros and the thylacine (the latter being the Tasmanian tiger; Benjamin, suspected of being the last one in existence, died in captivity in 1936).

In the long history of humanity, over thousands of generations, there's an undeniable sequence. Wherever there's human evolution, settling new territories or expansion through economy and industry, extinctions seem to happen or ecosystems suffer. It's surely time to create a new pattern.

When I think about space, the space race or the legacy of all scientific advances, such as the moon landing, I find myself thinking it's the bit in the middle that's truly fascinating. By that I mean the inner space: the curiosity, vision and innovative advancement that opened the doorway to the heavens. And our ability to ask ourselves a Shakespearean-style question to keep ourselves in check: 'to wreck or not to wreck?' Sure, not everything that pours out from our innovations is perfect but we, as a species, have the potential to retain the best breakthroughs amid a continual evolution while putting the less desired to rest, as if lost in space, on permanent ice—if we've got any ice left to put them on, that is.

I think if there's a legacy we could take from the moon landing 50 years on, it's this quote from Neil Armstrong: 'I believe every human has a finite number of heartbeats. I don't intend to waste any of mine'.

That sounds like great advice from a great member of humanity and one of only 12 people to date who walked on the moon with a chance to glance back some 384000 kilometres to the pale blue dot of our collective home.

Adding service value without waste, aligned with this fourth dichotomy, is knowing which technologies, discoveries, breakthroughs or knowledge *not* to adopt as much as which to use. The disruptions packaged as extinction rebellions also don't apply!

Inner-space service value is thinking globally even when acting locally. One community's waste is every country's worry. For far too long too many people, including corporations, have treated the planet and its resources like a no-holds-barred, endless-supply profit party. If we keep treating our environment in this reckless manner, then—a little like the GFC greed mentality—it's akin to saying 'last one to leave the planet on one of Elon's rockets gets to switch off the lights!'

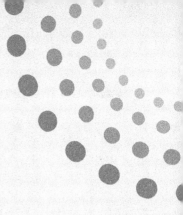

Service value
Tools, tips and self-reflEQtion

Take some time to ponder your impact in adding service value. For every choice and action taken (even at an individual level) with long-term solutions there is an equal reaction (somewhere in the world) playing out the possibilities and consequences for others, the environment and ourselves. Who knows, some momentum might impact a critical mass.

You may ignite a spark in your children to believe that anything is possible, that all they need is belief: a no-quit attitude combined with a dose of bravery to resolve, not merely complain about, inner-space global issues. If our future generations face the world radiating service value, imagine what could be achieved! (Although maybe no more extinction rebellions please.)

Complaining about things doesn't change them; consciously thought-out action does. To quote anthropologist Margaret Mead, 'Never doubt that a small group of thoughtful, committed citizens can change the world; indeed, it's the only thing that ever has'.

Here are some ideas. And don't forget to ponder other ideas—no doubt there are plenty—from situations playing out in your own life.

Process the problem differently

Catch the inner dialogues you're having. Where's your focus? Are you stuck on problem thinking? Analyse problems with the intent of understanding them, then 'flip the switch'. What are the purposeful, different questions you might ask?

Mastermind the problems

Who else can you ask for input in processing problems? Don't just rely on your friends—they will tell you what you want to hear. And make sure you ask people with credible input. Nobody is great at everything, so ask for quality input so you can get perspective on the root of problems in addition to quality solutions.

Love your job

Bryce Courtenay said, 'Superannuation is what we get paid for being bored for thirty years'. If that position, role or career is a countdown to superannuation, ticking essential boxes on the base steps of your needs pyramid, okay. But how can you find ways within the need to work to love what you do? Either love what you do or find a way to love elements of what you do. Our own happiness and the quality of the service we provide others significantly shift with this mindset alone.

Make amends

It's possible that parts of our past play on our minds. Yes, that one! Acknowledge it or, if possible, clean up your own mess. If you accidentally ran over someone, you would likely do your best to get them medical help rather than hit and run! The same is true in so many other, non-physical, situations. Taking responsibility and accountability frees you up.

Hit pause before you leap to decide

As a result of all those layers of human behaviour and personal value we may have a tendency to do one of two things: leap before we look or make choices based on preconceived ideas. Ponder a little longer the ongoing possibilities and consequences that may pan out.

Try walking in my shoes

Now imagine yourself in the shoes of the other party/parties impacted by your choices. What might have happened in their past to make them act or react to situations the way they do? How can you leave an indelible positive watermark rather than add an ugly stain?

Intentional activities for self and others

Find a hobby or participate in several with the only intention being that of finding your own bliss. What are some activities you've always wanted to try but have put off? Perhaps include them in the list. Then do the same to add to the joy of others.

Fingertip philanthropy: personal and professional

Identify causes you're passionate about or aligned with. How can you get involved? It may be offering some form of monetary or resource contribution, periodically volunteering, helping spread the word, or even just being a little more hands-on. Do the same with your own business or the business you work for.

Plant a tree, or adopt a pet

One of my mentors, Paolo Fortini—who has a chapter dedicated to him in my first book—gave me advice that there are three important things to do in a lifetime. One is to plant a tree. Trees are considered part of the functional lungs to our planet. So plant one, plant some or plant many. In this instance, planting a tree may be any initiative where environmental impacts are considered. It could be looking at your own footprint and waste, then finding ways to reduce them. It may also be to proactively cultivate a cause. And if you're going to get a pet, think about adopting a rescue!

5

Relationship value

The substance of life

One hundred and fifty.

Remember that number from when we deliberated those wonderful repetitive patterns locked in the code of nature? Well, 150 is another strange metric made relevant by the research of British anthropologist and psychologist Robin Dunbar.

While studying the behaviours of primate groups, he wondered why they spent so much time grooming and playing with one another. He began plotting playful preening time, group numbers and brain mass. He stumbled on an interrelationship synergy based on the common factor of brain size.

So what happened when he plugged the same findings into our own primate group to find out the number of relationships human beings can realistically maintain? He deduced that, based on the size of the human brain, the number is 150.

People generally find this number either not high enough or well overrated. Extroverted types (who may undertake endeavours by amassing an interconnected global village via tools such as social media) find the figure somewhat laughable. (I've even had people say unless you've hit a minimum benchmark of 1000 friends there must be something wrong with you!) Others who are a little more grounded, and a little more cautious of who they befriend, think they'd be lucky to even reach double digits in true meaningful connections.

So, in the manner of Leonardo da Vinci, let's dissect Dunbar's findings further. But don't worry: we'll be doing this analytically, without a cadaver or carved-up brain in sight. When Dunbar, and others, looked more closely across a broad spectrum of historical periods and other scenarios it turned out the number may have merit:

- average numbers within hunter-gatherer communities: 148

- average-sized English village circa 18th century: 160

- ideal church-sized congregations: <200

- average wedding guests (18000 brides in a 2008 study): 148

- modern military companies: approximately 150

- Gore-Tex's corporate infrastructure: approximately 150

- Facebook, average number of friends: 150–200

- Christmas card list networks: 153.5.

Yes, yes, if you're looking for evidence in numbers you'll surely find it. But the researchers' approach, as with any good science, was to do the study and see what they found—not like politicians spinning analysis to justify a theory. Which is another reason the number becomes so curious. The random nature and circumstances with which the number reveals itself is like an uncanny magician's trick where you want to know how the hell the researchers do it.

Forget the magic for a moment and think more practically about the realities of your own life. Assuming you have a Facebook page:

- How many of your virtual 'friends' do you actually really know?

- How many might you cut off without warning if you felt so inclined?

- How many cut you off without you knowing for a long time?

- How many, if they pass you in the street, could you recognise and name?

- How many are you in regular, meaningful contact with?

The answer to that last question, according to Dunbar, is that we may spend more than half of our time, as much as 80 per cent, talking to the same handful of friends. Which is likely to be as few as five. Think again about your own world for a moment before you decide! The trouble with digital is that it clumps every Tom, Dick, Harry or Sam the serial stalker into one happy bucket. A short-term dopamine fix of fake, fluffy loveliness called 'friends'. We can look at our world rather in circles to get a sense of where that meaningful line, like a passport border may live:

- tight inner circle, family, having earned the right or your choice

- extended family and friends including happy, fun 'aunties and uncles'

- your or your parents' friends who know too much (you gotta keep 'em close)

- other fans who may cry if you're hurt or you die (but who may laugh at any slight misfortune)

- career friends who may also sneak into the heart and inner social circles

- career friends you'll happily hang out with on Fridays

- career contacts you'll politely hang out with but... 'Who was that again?'

- local shop owners and periodic suppliers

- neighbours we love who get an invite to the barbecue or wedding

- neighbours we can't wait to see move away

- transient friends we see periodically and happily pick up with where we left off

- transient friends from travels we promise to catch up with but never do

- digital friends—all of the above, plus ones you stumble on who you think look hot

- digital friends—all of the above, plus so many randoms you haven't got a clue.

Many of these subgroups live in isolation. Some cross-pollinate, collide or tick a few simultaneous boxes. But if you were to scribble down your own lists, how many would you see as being meaningful? How many would qualify for that curious Christmas card list of 153.5? Perhaps the neighbours, depending on how loud they play the drums and whether they manage to keep their yapping dog away from your cat.

An annual salutation prompted by an automatic birthday reminder hardly measures up as the basis for an idyllic relationship. A random click on a mass-marketed thumb—no comment—even less so, surely? And when you hear about infighting and backstabbing from apparent allies, no longer is the relationship not meaningful, it also negates the very meaning of 'friends'.

Dunbar shares that there are two components of the brain—one just above the eyes and the other in the temporal lobe behind the ears—that form a sort of social-cognition circulatory system. This arms you with an ability to recognise and relate to other people and identify the emotional states of others. We've also learned from neuroscience of the brain's neuroplasticity—that is, its ability to adapt and change. We can affect, to some degree, the size of our neocortex brain and its abilities through activities such as rigorous training and cognitive exercise. That said, Robin Dunbar goes on to suggest that once you're in your early twenties, your ability to maintain meaningful relationships is pretty much capped out. No Facebook or Google algorithm can hack that. And any efforts to try to do that are futile.

The race for popularity and hyper-connection in the digital era may therefore actually detract from the quality of relationships that are, or have the potential to be, meaningful. You're just not equipped with the required hardware.

Back in those Neolithic villages, circa 6000 BCE, you'd likely interact with a group of 150 people or so your whole life. Sure, there were swapsies, but these were generally related to births, deaths or visitors—you know, vendors with tokens for trade (in modern times it may be the Russian guy in a bright, horrible Contiki shirt with a collection of dodgy CDs).

Nowadays people race to interact with the highest number of 'likes' that they can—far more than 150—within a minute of a social media post. Over the course of a longer lunch break or entire day they're aspiring for those 'friend' interactions to be in the thousands. It all goes against critical considerations or the science of Dunbar's evidence-based relationship value count. The irony is that 'Dunbar's number' became so-named through the world of stories trending in masses on digital media.

One important metric of who might qualify in your prime connected group of 150 is, in part, determined by the measure of time. If you don't invest time in relationships, they decay and fade away. Dunbar even found the average, real, intimate, close group number of friends we're connected with is five. Except for those in a close personal relationship: their intimate friend number fell to four. He cheekily suggests it's why we must be truly careful who we date, live with or marry because the price you pay may be the cost of a close friendship. Maybe this gives credence to the philosophy that you should indeed marry your best friend!

Of course, many contributing factors determine the overall quality of all our relationships. All those layers of human behaviour and personal value systems are at play. If you have a strong, active belief towards nurturing the planet it's less likely you'll hook up with or befriend someone who thinks ripping up the Great Barrier Reef for coal shipping laneways is a good idea. Well, unless they're hot—then you might invite them into your Facebook circle. But no way are they on the Christmas card list.

It's better to accept it's impossible to remain in close contact with all who cross our paths. People enter our lives for a reason, a season or a lifetime. Time, values and experiences cipher our interactions and people who cross our path, to help determine who belongs where, which is which, or even in what capacity. Regardless, you can make all interactions, no matter how minimal, ones of respect and value.

The complexities in the world of meaningful relationship connections, whether on digital platforms or in actuality, do have one thing in common. They're virtual.

Science tells us that relationships only exist in our imagination. So be mindful of where to invest your precious time. We construct them and give them meaning, and those meanings live in the imagination and the mind.

The virtual ones, chasing popularity or fame on social media, can be very troublesome—and are they really worth it? It often means battling to keep on the hedonistic treadmill of trending or fighting to stay on the right side of convoluted algorithms shuffled on a whim by profit-seeking strangers in Palo Alto. Or beneath the radar of trolls and hackers with way too much time on their hands who are shitty because they have significantly fewer than five real friends (unless other trolls with the same values count).

Perhaps some of your precious time is better redistributed to the intricate workings of the virtual relationship technology that's been formed over thousands of years: your brain linked with a virtually indestructible chord to your chest: 'First with the head, then with the heart', as Peekay from Bryce Courtenay's *Power of One* would say. Which people in that circulatory loop really matter? Invest quality time into those relationships to keep them safe as a part of your tribe.

There's also the strange phenomenon of relationship chemistry. Some people find their way quickly, annoyingly or scarily (at times) into your heart and mind. Then, no matter how hard you try—not the passage nor circumstance of time—they remain an imaginary relationship engrained on the brain. Possibly for a lifetime! The memory of them alone lingers to haunt that circulatory loop. Likely top 10 even! Sometimes we relegate people who care about us, who are genuine and valuable, blocking them from our circle of 150 people. And instead invest the valuable time it takes to maintain relationships on less worthy candidates, the people who treat us badly. The tangible measure of Dunbar's number is the actual friend zone.

I'm sure pondering all this talk of friends, relationships and cosmic connections may spark musings of the likes of Rumi or Paulo Coelho. They can wait for a moment. Both will surface shortly amid the depth of the four traits of relationship value, the topic of this chapter.

However, if you're itching for a teaser it was Coelho who observed that 'important encounters are planned by the souls long before the bodies meet'. But if there were a trump hand amid them, assuredly the next four traits are aces. To ignore, forget or take them for granted is to run the risk of tossing aside rare, real, precious people—gems from the stream of life. You miss them, you see. Or simply can't appreciate their worth as you're far too busy wasting your time rummaging in the shallows collecting more common pebbles, rocks and shells.

Relationship value in a nutshell

The four traits of relationship value are perhaps the equivalent of an ace hand if value were dealt like cards:

1. Authenticity: an original you
2. Candour: the biggest dirty little secret
3. Kindness: random and conscious acts
4. Love: the meaning of life

1. Authenticity: an original you

In this digital era, a concept once meant to inspire tenacity and grit for people to step up has taken on a whole new life. 'Fake it till you make it', taken literally, has turned social media into another cryptocurrency.

The tangible value metrics, engagement volumes, reviews or ranks are the equivalent of paper dollars; while the totals of thumbs or other emojis, along with bulk numbers in views or followers are the more annoying jingling coins. Then add 'stories', instant videos and photos as a symbolic plethora of selfies acting as tokens. Combined, they bolster the new currency of social proof, exploding with propensity as part of a new bartering system vying for free trade.

If you give me stuff, all sorts of goods and services—5-star hotel stays, first-class flights, fine dining restaurant meals, branded clothing or even guest spots on blogs and other mainstream media—in return I'll give you goodwill and visibility. I'll stamp your business with appropriate symbols in hashtags as guest spots on my token selfies. You're bound to get more trade.

So let's put this currency, as with all historical fiscal forms, through the necessary filters required for legitimisation. Let's check the sustainability or validity. While a couple of easier boxes have been ticked, it's the more critical ones we need to look at closely:

- *Durable.* ✓ Anything whacked up on digital follows you around for life.

- *Effortless to carry.* ✓ Everywhere, all the time, like an extra limb.

- *Legal.* ✓ Hell yeah! Everybody's doing it, we're still in the early days in the wild west.

- *Hard to forge.* ✗ Not by a long shot! Things start to come badly unstuck.

Take Oobah Butler as a classic case study. Butler, an author, journalist and film-maker born in 1992, represents Gen Y, millennials, next gen and beyond. Using a tongue-in-cheek rascal's approach he continually highlights flaws and how easy it is to commit fraud within digital media.

At one point he was being paid to write fake reviews for restaurants on TripAdvisor to elevate rankings. It gave him an inspiring idea. Could he turn a non-existent location into one that might be verified? He created a website featuring plated foods (using common household products, like shaving foam or dishwashing tablets!), then secured a dedicated phone number. He turned a hut where he pretty much lived in Dulwich, south of London, into the dining spot known as The Shed.

Butler clearly understood the relevance of emotional value given he utilised thought-out content copy positioning the eatery as wonderfully unique: *Instead of meals, our menu is comprised of moods.*

An extended circle of friends continually posted fake reviews. By November 2017, less than seven months after opening, this weird gustatory fiction, existing only in cyberspace, had garnered momentum. The Shed had reached the number one spot in London on TripAdvisor. Butler, keen to take it one step further, decided to give eager diners a live experience. So he figured 'what the hell' and opened up for a single night.

Packaging the evening as a press night, attendees weren't charged. He had actors planted to ensure a bona fide perception, along with other guests including international travellers, foodies and bloggers. They were served cheap microwave meals. Butler thought he'd be busted for sure, especially as a few looked sombre throughout the event. You can imagine his surprise and delight when he found that some wanted to book again!

Encouraged by the project's success he replicated the experiment with a different product. Purchasing several pairs of street-brand jeans, 'Georgio Peviani', he adopted the persona of Georgio, the designer. He successfully bullshitted his way through security checks and networks to be given passes during Paris Fashion Week. Peviani was to become the toast of the town. Again, influencers and buyers requested product procurements and prestigious catwalk forums opened their doors. He took these successes back to the UK where he tracked down the owner of the actual registered high street brand label. He'd built them a new base of popularity, insta-famous style sales, to build upon. Butler received awards from the LA Fashion Festival and the British Society of Magazine Editors for these efforts, including the British Media Awards's 'Video Project of the Year' for 2018.

Finding himself bored with media interview requests and always looking for the next hilarious hoax, Butler then decided to fake himself. He sent proxies and stand-ins to a variety of local and international appearances with an unwitting media. His own brother successfully adopted his character, passing the test—albeit by video link—on Australia's *Weekend Sunrise* program. They didn't even pick him as a sibling. He just sat there smiling while being told by the hosts how wonderful it was to have him back. Oobah had made a personal appearance only a year before.

When Butler featured on live television during fever pitch of 'The Shed' incident, host Susanna Reid from *Good Morning Britain* probed him with a valuable question: 'In order to garner something real from the experiment, how do you see through fake information?' Butler's response was, 'We're at a point where truth is overrated on internet websites now'. Surely this busts the myths and value of social proof currency. While Reid chastised him in a motherly fashion—Monty Python's *Life of Brian* style—as a very naughty boy, I think Butler is more of a jester king. He didn't perpetuate lies with malice but rather to hold up a mirror for all to see the absurdities of what's considered worthy in the digital age.

Fake it till you make it (or you fall)

We're living in a society that goes beyond fake reviews. Where a rush for fame or fortune explodes the aphorism 'fake it till you make it' into an unscrupulous ethos in the hands of phony personas. These conmen and women willingly operate under the same ideology that birthed Nazi Germany's Third Reich. Adopting methods of 'Große Lüge'—the big lie—they know people these days are too busy or distracted seeking their next fix. Any patience previously invested into valuable diligence goes the way of the dodo. Popularity or celebrity, often self-proclaimed, then takes on a life of its own. Escalating rapidly, all too frequently stratospherically, social currency is confused for credibility or even basic capability. Barely a day goes by when we're not exposed to more diabolical swindles.

In Australia we're aware of people like Belle Gibson. She faked surviving cancer to procure corporate support to promote her *The Whole Pantry* app and cookbook. She was featured in a plethora of popular culture magazines and milked a small fortune into her own profitable pantry before being exposed as a fraud. She even failed to follow through on charitable donations and treated her fines and punishment with contempt.

An even more startling story is that of Elizabeth Holmes, who became a poster child for a new kind of university dropout: a young, female entrepreneur with a vision of disrupting established fields of medicine. As founder of Theranos, she became a *Forbes* magazine cover girl and TED speaker with an enviable board of accomplished directors. The business climbed to the lofty height of a fiscal valuation of approximately $9 billion—the only problem being that the whole science of taking a single pinprick of blood to figure out all one's health woes was a sham.

Holmes was an avid admirer of Steve Jobs. Whereas Jobs was known as a straight shooter, Holmes reeked of inauthenticity, replicating a public persona rife with similar mannerisms to that of her hero: dressing in a consistent uniform—a turtleneck top—for media appearances, along with a questionable baritone voice. She even hired several previous key senior Apple employees.

That's not to say Holmes's story started out as a deliberate dupe. No doubt the doe-eyed schoolgirl believed such a scientific breakthrough was possible. To challenge established models is how we propel society forward. The problem is choosing to continue when it becomes clear your aspirations are in reality more a dream, like Dorothy's after clicking her little red heels in *The Wizard of Oz*. To continue the deception becomes deplorable: it's a path of optimism turned to egotism turned to crime. The title of the documentary *Out for Blood in Silicon Valley*, released at the 2019 Sundance Film Festival, is a perfect idiom for an objective view. The shambles of blood in broken machines reiterates the current state of play in society, which enables dubious personalities to elevate in plain sight.

Splattered haemoglobin is a perfect symbol for how inauthenticity morphs into a bloody mess when we're too eager to thrust people on pedestals.

Frank Abagnale, the real-life fraudster made famous by Leonardo DiCaprio in the film *Catch Me If You Can* warned that despite conning millions over 40 years as a fake pilot, doctor and lawyer, in today's digital age he would have cleaned up.

So before leaping, via virtual signalling or hamming up your personal brand, take time to hit pause. Delve a tad deeper like an amateur detective. Then ask better questions. Some people may always slip through the net (hey, Lance Armstrong!). But a little assiduousness may keep you more alert to the subtleties of real folk versus scams. Should you find exemplary merit in a perceived role model, figure out what precisely it is that's worthy of such applause. How might you replicate, not duplicate, this? In a natural, comfortable and ethical style aligned with the layers of your own personal value? An original you is way more valuable than a carbon copy.

Know thyself and find your flow

The role of a leader developing others is to help them learn earlier than they otherwise might the pitfalls they may face or the error of their own ways while simultaneously coaxing the best version of the students themselves to emerge. When I was training tour leaders to deliver that million-dollar experience of a lifetime I understood this well. My job wasn't to produce a bunch of mini-mes.

- There were those—high dominance—ones, who might resolve challenges and issues quickly but perhaps be perceived as a little too direct, standoffish or cold.

- Others—the high influence ones—might be the life and soul of the party: fun big picture dreamers with a knack for great storytelling and spontaneous fun.

- Others—high steadiness—were more likely armed with an inbuilt sense of empathy and collaboration, thus they would more easily harmonise their entire group.

- And some—high compliance, the quiet achievers—were best armed not to miss a beat in the complexities of organisation but did so less in the spotlight.

The same is true when developing authentic paths of success in business arenas such as leadership or operations. Sales is always a good example.

- There are those who ooze a strong confidence, who keep their clients on track and up to date. Clients will respect their logic and tenacity enough to sign the dotted line but may find them a little too direct or pushy at times.

- Others will be like a playful retriever. Give them so much as a sniff of an opportunity and they'll find a way, even through scrub or bush, to go fetch. Just keep an eye on administration oversights, errors or paperwork to be tidied up.

- Others have customers they bond with who will then follow them no matter where they go. If people only bought the best-recognised products, this wouldn't be so. But, we buy from people, as we do the product or service at hand.

- Then there are the folks beavering away leveraging significant chunks of time to depth of details—proving undeniable capability or strong ROI. This may mean volumes in sales activities are less than hunting dogs chasing bones.

You can apply the same thinking to an arena like comedy. It's one field of entertainment where there's a definitive outcome: make me laugh out loud. Comedians mastering their craft achieve this result, leveraging the layers of personal value authentically:

- Ricky Gervais, taking no prisoners, willingly, ruthlessly pisses off or embarrasses industry peers at occasions such as hosting the Golden Globes.

- Sir Billy Connolly CBE has carved out a career as a meandering storyteller. He'll begin several anecdotes yet somehow tie them all up neatly with a bow.

- Graham Norton created forums for giggles where the laughter lies in the gift of his own gab bouncing off celebrity guests for amplification.

- Jerry Seinfeld is a diligent researcher and calibrator: in his comedy, every second, syllable or word has earned its place through trial and testing.

All incite laughter via an authentic path. For example, if comedy were a science, Jerry Seinfeld would be the academic professor sharing findings with stealth in a refined language of finesse. Seinfeld even says if he were to be played just the laughs from his sets he'd be able to tell you, from chuckles alone, what the joke was. Such is his diligence to understanding his craft.

While millennials and later generations are targeted the most with the digital addiction infliction of having your head constantly buried in a phone, the phenomenon crosses all generations. In fact, the worst offenders for inauthenticity, portraying life through carefully selected filters as perfection, were born decades before any reality television stars bolstered their family name into a cash cow. Some people have spent a lifetime cultivating a public persona hiding in the shadow of the Dunning–Kruger effect, whereby people overestimate their genius or skills when they're likely average. There's a clue in how *The Washington Post* labelled Oobah Butler the 'Donald Trump of TripAdvisor'.

Personally I find millennial and next gen audiences a little more present. When encouraged to put phones down for submersion into content of personal value and behavioural layers, they lap up the opportunity. Perhaps having fewer years with which to harbour biases, fixed mindsets or stubborn beliefs, they find the content fascinating. It's as if life's hidden secrets are finally being revealed. One example I love springs to mind:

Oh! This explains so much! I get it now! I was pretending to be really, you know, like emo [emotional] and stuff. Because the hot guy everybody liked was, you know, really deep. Anyway, it worked! I got with him! But then after a while it didn't work. Because, you know, we're just not that alike.

An authentic persona from the land of TED Talks, notably an expert on the subject, must surely be the wonderful Brené Brown PhD, who declares that 'Authenticity is a daily practice'.

Authenticity takes courage. The courage to be honest with yourself and others. The courage to be vulnerable. There's great strength in allowing the world to see those things about ourselves we deem to be weaknesses or flaws.

The courage to let go of the masks. The courage to stop pretending to be something we're not because it's what we feel is expected of us or simply to fit in. Or when we feel we're not good enough.

As Brené Brown says, 'We are all made of strength and struggle'. Authenticity in the current age is embracing all of it, not portraying a life through filters. It's when we embrace authenticity that we invite gratitude and grace into our lives.

Inauthenticity wielded willy-nilly tends to be like the hyperinflation of bust economies. The more you're pushing around in a wheelbarrow the less value you're likely to find.

Authenticity, on the other hand—owning your mistakes and embracing the opportunity to turn up as your best, warts and all—is a powerful causation inviting or adding value into our lives and the lives of others.

If I were a trial lawyer addressing a court delivering a summation on the importance of this trait, with Elizabeth Holmes or someone like her in the dock, right about now is where I'd say, 'I rest my case, Your Honour'.

2. Candour: the biggest dirty little secret

Silence, which I shared in earlier chapters, through ostracism and playground bullying for being a 'f*cking Sassenach', has been a major entire-life lesson. It turns out I was learning about it from the day I was born courtesy of two grandfathers.

Grandad number one taught me how to play cards. He'd hustled as a young man to make a few extra dollars as a side living. He then passed this skill in reading and playing your hand most appropriately on to me. Not in the art of gaming or the habit of gambling, but as lessons in personal growth. The cards and poise in how to play them were a metaphor for principles associated with the ebbs of life and subtleties of human behaviour.

When dealing with someone skilled at being poker faced you become more adept at reading the stakes and mind games going on. Cards also teach such things such as patience and acceptance. You may not be able to foresee or choose the cards you're being dealt. What you can learn is the appreciation of their potential, even when dished out in what may seem a poorer hand. The skill in how to play them is all within your own resolve.

He was adamant that how someone may choose to participate with intent to win, playing a fair and square game or cheating, indicates the true nature of their character. He was raised to realise the importance of wishing others well when they won. To be genuinely happy for them, wishing them the very best regardless whether such luck seemed fortuitously to fall in their lap, either by being dealt a better hand or through smart calls and cunning confidence. Wishing others prosperity was important because to do so demonstrates humility and a greater understanding of the wider capacity and nature of the wheel of life. At some stage winning smiles over a big pot may wane, as the same people face folding where equal fortunes just as easily fall. Grandad number one was the card-playing philosopher.

Then there's Grandad number two. He also played cards in his youth. He was from Chesterfield. He met and married my grandmother. He left my grandmother. Later in life he lived on the remote island of Tiree off the west coast of Scotland. And that's about as much as I know. In fact, it was only when I was about 19 years old that I discovered all this when we were told a visitor was swinging by.

When the stranger turned up he looked uncannily like my father. He was cool, level-headed, calm and kind. It took a wee while for my brain to compute the guest playing cards and drinking tea was actually my grandfather. It wasn't stated outright. I'd always been led to believe this particular grandparent had passed away before I was born. After meeting him for this first time in Edinburgh, I was fortunate to spend a little more time with him. I took a road trip to the windswept isolated island of Tiree, population 700, with my own father. It was time well spent, as it wasn't very long after this trip that my grandfather finally did pass away.

Grandads one and two are the same man. The first version is the slight wisdom I may have weaned from him, wrapped in a little fiction. As we know, memory stores what it wants to in details and then embellishes accordingly. I can't recall the facts or all the details. I do remember trying to play golf on the island, with winds dragging balls or holding them up. It was a nightmare. But I also know while playing cards with him by his bedside that the feeling of his character was spot on.

My philosophical card-playing grandfather was exiled from our lives, zero access, before I was born. Whatever did or didn't happen depends on whose version of events you listen to. That's not a judgement. It's just a fact. Clearly for me when a grandfather figure who I'd always believed to be dead turns up, curiosity emerges purely out of interest. Questions proved a little difficult to answer or were perceived as curve balls by some of those invested or wounded parties.

Then, depending again on the person addressing them, their answers may be curt, ambiguous or justifiably spun. The black and white answers from each party's recollections didn't reconcile into an easy single story or version. Again, that's not a judgement. I get it. It's the layers of personal value, the meaning-making machines at play, sorting out their own version of life.

My grandmother maintained she never wished her son, my father, to isolate his own parent or to deny him access to any of us. My father would say he felt such a course of action was implied. That a sense of duty, loyalty or respect for his own mother meant any other decision would have been more difficult once chosen, or as consequences unfolded, more difficult to be undone. A clean break therefore had to be made. My grandfather didn't really say much on the other subject. Sweeping it aside, he maintained he always respected the decision and only wished he'd had a chance to be a bigger player in his son's and our lives.

I do find it ironic that my grandfather, being excommunicated, should find solace and peace settling with his partner in such an isolated environment. He had made a significant effort to keep the door open. Apparently, presents from 'Santa' turned up each year with no explanation as to which Santa or why. It's likely this patience and persistence for what turned out to be virtually the remainder of his life, bar a few months, was the key finally nudging open a pretty firmly closed door.

I guess somewhere beneath the stubbornness of what he was being faced with he'd played enough hands of cards in his life to know that every door, even firmly locked ones, are somehow slightly ajar. When the chips are down and all is lost your hand may yet be successfully turned around.

I'm glad I met my paternal grandfather. He passed away from a heart condition shortly after my Tiree trip. The storyteller in me learned enough in those few days to turn bedside convalescence conversations into nuggets of non-fiction gold. It also provided awareness of a different manner as to why some people ostracise and cut ties that has nothing to do with the target being a f*cking Sassenach.

My father chose a course of action and stuck with it. Yet I also now know, having finally taken down those self-imposed walls, he felt the gap and absence. I find further irony echoed in his own life. As he ages, not in particularly great health at the time of writing, he finds himself in similar isolation. Not in terms of a remote destination, but in regard to emotional isolation from relationships, family and friends. It's certainly not a deliberate exile on anyone's part. It's just how life has turned out. That isolation, also ironic, likely began in earnest after a separation and divorce from my mother, which was the very same situation that drove him to excommunicate his own father. The difference though is none of us have deliberately cut him off. I know my father wouldn't necessarily agree and feels at times people don't make the effort. In my case, to some degree, working for so many years in the travel industry and settling halfway around the globe, there's some truth. I'm not the son or the sibling to make regular phone calls. My mother too knows this well and there have been periods where we may go months without conversation. That said, when it comes to my father and my siblings who still reside in the UK, along with my nephews, they do make and take the time to phone and visit. If he's feeling isolated, a lot of it has been a result of continued choices, habits and actions perhaps spanning back years.

Too often many people ignore straight-shooting, difficult conversations. Or with a fixed mindset they push others' perspectives to one side. It's said that water in all its states is the archetypal dream symbol for emotional states. With this being the case, any difficult conversations avoided keep trickling, out of sight, as quiet mountain streams of bad blood. With the passage of time and distance they flow into wider rivers then larger obstructing dams. Dams can only handle so much capacity before, one way or another, as a necessary staged release or unexpected flood from destruction, the dam's capacity will break. Either way, years of harboured feelings then flood out in torrents.

A lack of candour is a killer

Something my father—who joined the Royal Navy at a young age and spent more than 20 years in service—recently shared on reflecting his own mortality was poignant: 'I spent most of my younger years on the sea. Then, since leaving the navy, I realise I've spent the remainder of my life completely out to sea'.

In the ensuing years, from being a 'f*cking Sassenach' at the age of five, rediscovering a grandparent at 19 to now being 50-odd years old, my close acquaintance—silence (sometimes archangel, sometimes nemesis)—has accompanied me the whole way.

Some of the easier situations in handling silence pertain to my business or career. Political spins and politics have meant on three separate occasions, with periods totalling close to 17 years, corporate farewells have been hastened or non-existent.

In a separate, specific incident, a couple of business contacts cut ties completely without explanation despite having been well-established friendly connections. I endeavoured without success to speak with them. Which only leaves curious inner contemplation. What could I have done? The only thing that sprang to mind was my open support at the time for gay marriage. Perhaps those contacts held values I wasn't aware of—like Israel Folau—so perhaps rather than have any discussion they chose to board up shop and run. I could think of no other reasons for shunning. And that's cool. But that's also just a story, a meaning I've come up with because the truth is I haven't got a clue. But if they don't tell me I can't do anything about any slight I may have unwillingly caused in order to make amends.

In his book *Winning*, Jack Welch describes this inability to have straight-shooting conversations—this lack of candour—as 'the biggest dirty little secret in business'. I just love that moniker. If you're not familiar with Jack Welch, he was chairman and CEO of General Electric for 20 years between 1981 and 2001. During his tenure, the company's value rose by approximately 4000 per cent. His retirement payout, a tad shy of half a billion dollars, is one of the largest severance handshakes in history. A straight-shooter himself, it's easy to see why Jack strived to embed the philosophy of candour and openness in all companies under his umbrella.

Welch says, 'What a huge problem it is! Lack of candor basically blocks smart ideas, fast action, and good people contributing all the stuff they've got. It's a killer'—the reason being it's no easy feat when you're going against people's long-held personal value layers, behaviours and life experiences. Honesty can be a little unnerving. Directness, sometimes too much so, may just as easily be given meaning and mistaken for aggressive confrontation.

Welch continues,

> When you've got candor, and you'll never completely get it, mind you—everything just operates faster and better. A lack of candor does not necessarily equate to malevolent dishonesty. It can just mean withholding constructive criticism, or keeping your opinion to yourself to make people feel better and avoid conflict.

More than fostering a mindset of straight-shooting business talk, I've come to learn that being ignored in school grounds must have armed me, slightly, with a tolerance-like mithridatism: the practice of building up immunity and protection against being exposed to or being continually administered specific poisons in non-lethal amounts. If it doesn't kill you, it makes you stronger!

If it weren't for being smacked about as a 'f*cking Sassenach', then ostracised in the kids' version of silent treatment I might have found the adult version, ghosting, a little more noxious or pernicious. One way or another, I've had enough silent treatment in 50-odd years to last several lifetimes.

The phenomenon known as ghosting

Whether you're candid or candour resistant, the ghost or the ghostee, the ignorer or the ignored, here are some succinct straight-shooting insights to avoid building up your own dams from streams of bad blood.

Candid conversations are an opportunity to speak your mind and are critical in the maintenance of all relationships. As Dunbar highlighted, where there's no quality time spent in communication, the relationship value decays. Remember those nuances of personal value may be at play. In any disagreement, misunderstanding or conflict there are two primary types of response:

- *Person A* prefers to talk it out now: let's thrash out a resolution

- *Person B* prefers you to go away, give them space and let them come back to you.

Both are correct. Take the high ground: attempt to give the other party what they need. Doing so may disarm the tensions or fears that lie beneath. They may sound something like this.

- *Person A:* 'I know you'd prefer some space. So I'll go away for a while. Please let me know when you're ready as my brain may be doing loops in the meantime'.

- *Person B:* 'I know you'd prefer to talk about this. I just need some space. I promise I'll come back after some time out' (be sure to follow through).

If you find yourself *on the receiving end of silent treatment* there's no need for anger. Process your own grief and move to a state of acceptance swiftly. It's okay. You'll survive. Life experiences, remember! The other party surely has their reasons and until they decide to tell you, try not to give it meaning or judge. I've also been flawed in my own communications with others. We all may want to hide in our caves when our vulnerabilities or insecurities are on display for the world to see. Or where the memories of pains and previous experiences feel pressed upon like unhealed wounds. If you must self-reflect, here's a few possible contenders to find and reclaim your own inner calm:

- You've done something to upset them somehow; reflection may help hone in.

- If you know you've done something, apologise sincerely then leave them alone.

- The person has other things going on in life you don't know about.

- It's got absolutely nothing to do with you.

- The person has a fear, perhaps of hurt or abandonment, so this is a defence.

- Indifference, life and times change swiftly and connections peter out.

- They are using silence as a form of keeping in control.

- In extremes, it may be a deliberate weapon of control: narcissism.

If you find *yourself dishing out the silence* again pause and ponder the choices. There may be a healthier course of action. Unless you're a narcissist or indifferent (in which case, I guess, atomic bombs away!) consider the consequences and possibilities of such choices. Any deliberate avoidance of difficult conversations, like those streams of bad blood, may still build up. It's *your own dam that overflows in torrents or breaks one day*:

- If someone has upset you, tell them; they may not know and can't guess.

- Allow space for an apology, then, if need be, have a clean parting of ways.

- The person has other things going on in life affecting their choices. They may be acting out of character.

- It's got absolutely nothing to do with you but you may want to ask.

- If you have fears, do they have validity; don't be a prisoner to your past.

- Be mindful not to punish present friends for others' errors.

- Silent treatment as a weapon can be no better than physical assault.

- If you're a narcissist, then, I guess, atomic bombs away.

Ostracism—the silent treatment—and a lack of candid conversation have been shown in research to impact neural pathways in the victim in a similar sequence as that triggered by physical pain. Put another way, to deliberately and consciously ostracise or ignore people is no better than physically assaulting them. Silent treatment can be a nastier weapon. While cricket-bat cuts heal, a lack of candour may leave invisible scars.

In my own TEDx Talk I shared a perspective on an African tribe, the Babemba, referenced by Alice Walker (social activist and novelist of *The Colour Purple*) and self-help author and speaker Dr Wayne Dyer. When someone in the tribe acts irresponsibly or unjustly, they are placed in the centre of a circle. The rest of the village gathers around and each tribe member address the accused, one at a time, only recalling and reminding them of the good deeds and behaviours they had previously conducted in their lifetime. The candid focus is to instil the positive attributes. Some say the tradition is based on a mixture of ideas from different tribes rather than one alone. Others allude to an exaggerated fiction. Regardless, the story has gone viral on more than one occasion because there's something in it we know inherently appeals: speaking squarely and justly yet with an attitude and mindset to heal.

Candour and the counterbalance of appropriate silence are traits that work powerfully with the dichotomic choices we covered in the pursuit of service value: they may seed possibilities or consequences, create problems or deliver solutions. They can be like a super heroic weapon for good or used like a prison punishment sending people into dark despair. Candour can be delivered without malice.

The famous writer Mark Twain helps us understand the value of candour in a simpler life: 'If you tell the truth you don't have to try and remember anything'.

HRH the Dalai Lama implies its value as a fine force in the vein of Wonder Woman's lasso: 'In our struggle for freedom, truth is the only weapon we possess'.

Author Peggy Noonan reminds us of its value relative to Dunbar's number, for all entering our circle: 'Candour is a compliment; it implies equality. It's how true friends talk'.

If only French generals had been equipped to cut through their emperor's ego. Several of them in his face might have made a difference: 'Erm. Are you sure about this, Emperor? Napoleon? Bonie old boy! Do you know how damn cold Russian winters are and how sneaky those ruddy Cossacks can be?'

3. Kindness: random and conscious acts

In 2016, Philanthropy Australia found a touch over 80 per cent of the population gave a combined total of AU$12.5 billion to charities and not-for-profit organisations. A comparative study in the United States a year earlier estimated a little over 70 per cent of its population making donations with a collective value of US$373 billion (AU$540 billion). If value were really about business mindset—return on investment—that doesn't explain these volumes. What motivates people's decisions and choices?

The most common reasons cited for charitable donations included:

- alignment with values or cultural identity
- personal satisfaction and caring about doing the right thing
- giving back.

The reasons people cited for, then opted in to support, a specific cause or charity were:

- it's for a good cause
- respect for the work the particular charity or organisation conducts
- the contributor personally knows someone with a condition
- general sympathy for those in need and for those it helps.

Many of their findings match what we find with significant philanthropists such as Andrew Carnegie, The Gates Foundation and Chobani, aligning to themes of personal inspiration or interest.

Even some of their findings into reasons for non-contribution found some people prefer their philanthropic donation to be one of time, volunteering or resources in lieu of a fiscal contribution. The primary reasons people decide not to contribute comes down to a couple of chief concerns:

- I'm not in a position to give, can't afford to (base pyramid needs!)
- believing the government should be providing care through our taxes
- concerns about how much of the donation is lost to administration
- concerns about the privacy of contributors' information.

What's very clear is one thing: donations of vast sums, individual or business, aren't purely about a tax write-off!

There are businesses that strive to capitalise on the potent currency of positive PR, seen by the public and potential consumers in a favourable light as doing the right thing, at times jumping on the bandwagons of virtue signalling and trends. Often these backfire. The public may be naive at times with heroes they elect for pedestals, but not always by those beating the sound of their own drum.

That said, a large majority of philanthropy is conducted at a purer, non-PR, individual and anonymous level. Over 60 per cent of those singular contributors act in the spur of the moment, preferring spontaneous donations — which is a shame in some ways given that any planned contributions yield on average six times the amount.

There are two cautionary trends that stand out when comparing data patterns in contributions going back 10 years or more:

1. a slight decrease in numbers donating: 87 per cent to 80.8 per cent

2. fewer people wishing to donate higher amounts.

We can hypothesise as to why. There's quite a list of reasons. Let's start with some challenges from a collection side. As we know, the world is getting a little noisier; people's attention spans are getting a little shorter and the volunteers in the street giving time on behalf of their preferred charities have a harder time because of it. Separating many people's noses from their phones for long enough is no small feat. Plus, have you tried getting in between an influencer taking a selfie to give something up for nothing? They're often used to this equation being the other way around.

Then there are also challenges for those wishing to donate. Some are cautious in part due to the trends of fraudsters and tricksters. People, rightly, are a little more suspicious of being approached in the street cap in hand. There are also times when they find it difficult to navigate a main thoroughfare without the equivalent of a street market in collectors, petitioners or educators all battling to be heard above the noise.

Add it all together and we find the older methods of collection deliver less return for resources or effort than they once did. The same can be said about cold-calling phone campaigns.

Even in the digital arena, where people are willing to generously give, it doesn't get any less noisy. What with fights to support this or that cause for a million campaigns you find crowds offering funding aren't the only crowds you need to battle to cut through. Any person and their dog, or in the case of Israel Folau, his Bible, can set up a page.

The rugby player set up his own campaign after causing a stir in Australia that led to his dismissal from the sport. His lucrative career, which brought in approximately $1.25 million per annum in addition to lucrative sponsorships, ended after he suggested hell might wait for all sinners, including homosexuals. While Folau is entitled to his views, the fund page raked in over $1 million before the crowdfunding site GoFundMe decided to shut it down and reimburse donors. They saw the collection as violating the rights of others. While happy to foster campaigns for appropriate causes including welcoming diversity debates, they drew the line at being seen to back funding promoting discrimination of any kind. It's a fair call.

Folau may have taken early signs of his campaign more optimistically. He clearly had support from Christian groups. If he was really that concerned he could simply put a cap on, just not an Australian rugby one, snag some buckets from Bunnings then go run the gauntlet. He already knew people listened to his tweets so once his followers knew where to flock they could go throw in a few tokens. That's if they saw him or remained attentive running the gauntlet of generosity along with everyone else doing it tough on High Street.

Decades ago, the space for organisations you might consider making a philanthropic contribution to was simpler. The Benevolent Society is the oldest at over 200 years old. It has transformed from helping convicts and the poor to helping all Australians facing a broad array of challenges to live their best life. There are also more popular ones aligned with the culture and interests of Australians, such as Surf Life Saving or a number of cancer societies. There are global interests and brands such as the Australian Red Cross or Climate Council, and bodies that address specific challenges such as Beyond Blue, Mission Australia, The Smith Family or the Fred Hollows Institute, the latter being dedicated to the health and welfare of Indigenous Australians.

The space for orgs and charities is as busy as a stock exchange. In a research period in 2012, regulatory bodies granted registrations to some 8000 new charities. During the same time frame they simultaneously revoked or removed close to 13000 from the register.

Individuals perhaps become passionate about a cause. When we marry this with other trends, such as an increased noise about the importance of personal brand, having one's own org or charity may become appealing, even if set up with goodwill rather than for ego or fraud.

Warren Buffet could have set up his own structures. But he decided it best to virtually double the vast multibillion-dollar pot for philanthropic projects of the Bill & Melinda Gates Foundation. The establishment of a charity or 'not for profit' is no easy process. It may be worth considering alignment with respectable causes as a first point of call. You can still leverage the power of personal brand and do you really need your name on a label if the social motivation of donation is pure? Fewer contributions lost to admin or set-up means the Smiths, Freds and Surfies might have more power with their larger pools.

Giving is one of those human instincts hard wired into our DNA. In the Roko Belic documentary *Happy*, compassion was found to be a road that leads to happiness. Neuroscientist Richard Davidson, a professor in psychology, conducted studies with Matthieu Ricard, who was a subject of interest as a writer-turned-Buddhist priest who also happens to hold a PhD in molecular biology.

Scans of his brain while conducting compassion meditations found the parts associated with happiness or a reduction in mindset to negativity lit up as if on fire. The research was to earn Ricard a PR moniker he didn't particularly relate to or enjoy: 'the world's happiest man'.

In an interview that was shared by Britain's *Independent*, Ricard, shunning the compliment, asked the Dalai Lama if he could hibernate from the media attention. His Holiness responded, 'If they want you to be the happiest man, be the happiest man'. The wisdom in the message of compassion is more important than the messenger.

Joy and a feeling of fulfillment is a valuable part of our connection to others. *Happy* wisely points out we were content, or had the capacity to be happy, as a species before the internet, television or video games. Prior to that the same was true for fashion, electricity or cars. We don't need smartphones and thousands of friends bombarding our commentary with emojis to be happy. And if you do, then perhaps it's time to try a little cold turkey to break the addiction. Turn off tech, push through the cold sweats and seek first that fulfillment within.

Smiling and laughter influence happiness. They trigger a release of endorphins, an equal buzz of any opiate high. Where endorphins are induced, our tolerance for pain simultaneously increases. These findings are common across many studies, including those of our old friend—well, not officially given he's not in my 150—Robin Dunbar, who conducted his own research in the ideal location: live and in the thick of it at the famous Edinburgh Festival Fringe with comedians slating Sassenachs and the likes.

Compassion goes back to the earliest known tribes. Studies and theories of our cave-dwelling predecessors suggest they exhibited equally complex and essential traits in consideration of others:

- collaborating or hunting in packs, or gathering in groups, for the benefit of all

- huddling together in proximity to share warmth and resources
- living with their elders and collectively caring for the sick and young.

Common languages

These days we live on a planet with the 196 recognised countries we spoke of in chapter 2 (Tangible value). The number may be a little contentious with breakaway states vying for independence or situations like that of the masters of compassion originating in Tibet. Regardless, among the nations of the world there are close to 8000 known spoken tongues. Almost half the world's population claim one of the top 10 languages as their own mother tongue.

But the two common languages we all understand aren't in that top 10. The two common languages transcend the limitation or requirement to utter so much as a single spoken word. They don't require exacting symbols like that common adoption around the globe represented in numbers. The two common languages—kindness and love—may be acted upon subtly. Silently. Both are action based. Expensive words in fact lose value, or become completely worthless, when not backed up with congruency.

Kindness, with sincere contrition, has the power to cut through those uncomfortable silences or imposed excommunications of feuding families or friends. Acts of kindness are a language the deaf can hear and the blind can see. They have the power to bring light to the darkest of places. Kindness is inherent in our DNA.

As the science of fulfillment or happiness suggests—and as many a philanthropist and world game changer attest to—there's simplicity of truth in the words of the American 19th century philosopher Ralph Waldo Emerson: 'Happiness is a perfume you cannot pour on others without getting a few drops on yourself'.

Og Mandino authored *The Greatest Salesman in the World*, a book first published in 1968 and since translated into more than 20 of those global vernaculars. The small classic, part of my own essential book collection, tells the story (in the rags to riches archetypal style) of a poor camel boy achieving success and fulfillment. One of the reasons I love the book is the manner in which Mandino wrote it.

The book is structured for not only reading but also absorbing and then taking the time to invest the principles taught: 12 chapters, laid out in text as scrolls, to be read over a period and ratio of one a month. It takes time to translate learning into a new daily practice. In this digital world many may get fat consuming copious amounts of content. We may be less tenacious when it comes to translating those lessons into practical actions, habits and new norms. Mandino was all over kindness:

> Beginning today treat everyone you meet as if they were going to be dead by midnight. Extend to them all the care, kindness and understanding you can muster and do it with no thought of any reward. Your life will never be the same again.

Shakespeare is a source for one of the most outdated ideas of kindness. It is from Hamlet that we hear 'I must be cruel only to be kind'.

When you think about how messed up the idiom 'fake it till you make it' has become, perhaps we can better reframe this Shakespearean thinking using the second trait of relationship value. There are times it's important to 'be candid only to be kind'. Sharing truth with positive intent doesn't equate to the message being loved. Some recipients of candour may want to kill the messenger! Others may perceive candour as cruel depending on the meanings they give everything. But that's not the same as the intention behind any message. If you really believe you need to be cruel to people you may want to consider attendance at the next 'narcissists 'r' us' convention. Everybody gets 15 minutes on stage to share their top three traits, a unique personal trademarked hashtag plus a goody bag with an 'I am God' pin badge along with a sponsored mirror! Cruelty and kindness, like love and fear, reside at opposite ends of a spectrum. Candour and kindness co-exist.

A 1994 movie character became an unlikely icon as the epitome for demonstrating kindness over a lifetime—even in the face of adversity, under wrath or fire from others, long gaps of absence, avoidance and silence from those one cares about or loves. He also validates that the value of kindness has little to do with IQ or the size of one's purse (although he helped show how our wealth and ability to share even more substantially might vicariously improve through good karma later). His mother drummed into him in the early years, 'Remember what I told you Forrest. You're no different than anybody else is. You are no different'.

We never know the silent battles or demons that others face. Benchmarking personal challenges is not a competitive sport. Neither is benchmarking the size or effort in time or donations. So if we were sitting side by side, you and I, on a park bench, having this conversation about kindness, live, in person rather than vicariously via philosophical pages in a book, here's where I might be inclined to mimic the style of our unlikely illustrious hero, Forrest Gump: 'That's all I have to say about that'.

4. Love: the meaning of life

My favourite TED Talk is delivered in the quiet, warm, welcoming calm of an accomplished professor. He may not be a comedic academic like Seinfeld yet he shares a beautiful message with some humour.

Robert Waldinger is the fourth director of perhaps the longest study of adult life and development ever conducted. He's been at its helm since July of 2010.

The original studies began in 1938 with a group of 268 men. The ongoing research extended to 724 in the 1970s. The focus was on two distinctly different groups, the first being Harvard sophomores. The second were from Boston's poorest neighbourhoods. These contrasting standards of living or expectations of life make the enduring studies' findings all the richer.

I love how Waldinger jokes that as the years rolled by many of the Boston men, from poor areas or districts of tenements, later in life kept asking, 'Why do you wish to keep studying me when my life really isn't that interesting?' The Harvard men never asked that question.

The participants followed many paths and careers traversing all realms of blue- and white-collar workers and even the highest levels of political office. John F Kennedy, 35th President of the United States, was a part of the initial sophomore group.

The initial study peered into privileged lives hoping to discover clues to leading a healthy or happy life. The extended research of two cohorts of men, dissecting work, home and health from polar ends of society, morphed through decades into something far greater. The offspring of the initial groups, numbering more than 2000 children, were also invited for insight. Waldinger jokes again that when the wives were also formally invited into the research many said 'it's about time'.

Peering cradle to grave behind the curtain of private lives is definitely akin to *The Truman Show*. The insights are far more beneficial than entertainment voyeurism alone. The evidence-based findings on real emotion and human behaviour yield valuable relationship wisdom for us all. The research makes for a great Hollywood tale given it includes many, if not all, of the seven primary archetypal themes of storytelling you might find in a blockbuster:

- *rags to riches:* the climbing social ladders of success (and vice versa!)

- *overcoming the monster:* facing illness, or addictions such as alcoholism

- *mystery*: does anyone have a life without a few 'wtf's?

- *comedy*: the collection of research and interviews no doubt provided this

- *tragedy*: one might consider the assassination of JFK as such

- *rebellion and rebirth*: breakdowns in relationships or lost aspirations; some ventured to battle in World War II after studying

- *a quest*: it seems all found a precious treasure of wisdom over a lifetime.

In this case the quest culminates in valuable knowledge and caution. The treasure of the study can be summarised in three primary lessons culminating in a single priceless jewel.

Lesson 1: loneliness is a killer

It turns out social connections are great for us and loneliness kills. Those more socially connected to family, friends and community proved to be happier, physically healthier and (all things equal, in the absence of acts of God, accidents or assassinations) they lived longer.

As Waldinger says, 'The experience of loneliness turns out to be toxic', adding that those who are less connected are 'less happy' and 'their brain functioning declines sooner and they live shorter lives'.

Lesson 2: quality over quantity of connections

The real value of relationships is not the number of friends you have, or whether you're in a committed relationship or not. It's the quality of connections and relationships that matter. Hang on? Wait a moment! Say that again? It sounds remarkably like the wisdom garnered from Dunbar. So Robert's and Robin's studies, R&R, are very much on a par.

Robert (Waldinger) says:

It turns out that living in the midst of conflict is really bad for our health. High-conflict marriages, for example, without much affection, turn out to be very bad for our health, perhaps worse even than getting divorced.

He adds that, conversely, good, warm relationships make you feel protected.

One fascinating aspect of the study was that so much information had been harvested about the participants that when they were in their eighties researchers wondered if they could look back, pausing at the data in midlife to see if there were common predictive indicators as to who among them might turn out to be a 'happy, healthy octogenarian'. It turns out they could. And the health factor we tend to instantly reach for—elevated cholesterol level—was far less predictive in a happy ageing process than their satisfaction in their relationships. Close, warm, nurturing connections seem to buffer us from the burdens of ageing. Even in their eighties, those with physical pain remained happy even on days with elevated levels of pain. Those in unhappy relationships reported the opposite: pains escalating perhaps aligned with their emotions.

Lesson 3: good relationships buffer our brains and our bodies

Being in a secure attached relationship in your eighties is protective when the relationship is one you know you can count on. Those lucky enough to have found that are more likely to maintain sharpness of memory for longer. People in relationships with less confidence in reliance experience earlier memory decline.

This doesn't mean relationships are like the fiction of a Hollywood love story one might dream of. Relationships aren't always strawberries and cream. Human interactions—think about all those layers of personal value—can be misunderstood and somewhat messy. You don't need a Harvard degree to tell you that. Just ponder the petri dish of your own life experiences. Bickering and disagreement doesn't mean a relationship can't be healthy. There are times you've got to be candid to be kind. What's important is that beneath differing opinions, the other party is still someone you know and can rely on.

* * *

The single jewel is that feeling loved and supported is the answer. Love really does make the world go round it seems.

The three key findings are what Waldinger calls 'wisdom as old as the hills'. It's just that this amazing study with decades of tangible data, evidence-based knowledge, kind of backs it up. Words don't teach though. Life experience does. And at times, as we all know, we must fall on our swords, fall forwards, backwards at times, in order to learn. And let's not forget that important layer of behaviour: our *why*. Our drive and motivation in life will change due to milestones or circumstances.

Waldinger shared that in a survey of millennials asking about a multitude of important life goals 80 per cent answered 'getting rich' and a further 50 per cent 'the desire to be famous'. We see it playing out with the fascination in selfies and reality shows and the explosion of personal brands. Yet what's more fascinating is the same answers were true when the same questions had been posed to the initial Harvard sophomore cohort decades before.

For whatever reason, people often look at those being placed on pedestals—like the university drop-out who changes the world and makes billions in the process. They may believe the trappings of aesthetic beauty, consumerism, expensive toys or trophies are what you should chase to tangibly measure success in life. Worse still, replicating some of those behaviours from the very same people ultimately falling off podiums after turning out all too often to be lacking respect, courtesy or grace. Some of your heroes really aren't very nice when not faking it till they make it or putting on an inauthentic face for the media.

The reason I enjoy Waldinger's TED Talk is because his message hits home that family feuds, ostracism, hate, anger and friends bickering all take a toll. And the price is hefty. Often the anger or hate intended for someone else means constantly drinking the toxin yourself. I'd encourage you to watch Waldinger's TED Talk for more detail. Plus the way he closes his 12-minute message is a wonderful lightning bolt to hit it all home.

It must be love ... or is it?

Depending on your source of research you'll find many forms of love attributed by ancient philosophers. Some of the more common ones include:

- *eros:* erotic, sexual, passionate love
- *ludus:* playful love
- *pragma:* long-lasting or practical love
- *philia:* a deep friendship underpinned by love
- *philautia:* self-love
- *agape:* selfless love including a love for strangers.

Many of the psychiatrists and professors referenced throughout the book in earlier chapters vicariously explored love by default as a result of their work. Freud's theories, some psychologists may still be inclined to agree, alluded to the intertwining of love and sex as both a great strength and weakness. Maslow believed those people reaching self-actualisation on the highest steps of the pyramid were the people most capable of love.

Robert Sternberg, Professor of Human Development at Cornell University, asserts a concept—although not in the manner the typical label of 'a love triangle' provokes:

- *intimacy:* closeness and connection in a loving relationship
- *passion:* physical attraction and sexual consummation
- *decision and commitment:* for both short- and long-term love.

The three components, to various amounts and degrees, interact with one another. Greater levels of passion may lead to greater levels of commitment. Greater levels of commitment may lead to increased levels of intimacy. The extended model with the presence of one, two or all elements, generates combinations forming eight kinds of love. Kind of like a 'cootie catcher': a paper fortune-teller constructed origami style, labelled with numbers, patterns or colours, concealing different messages beneath its flaps. You may recall it from the school playground (and there's probably an app for that now too).

The cootie-catcher's flaps would read:

- *liking:* intimacy alone

- *infatuation:* passion alone

- *empty love:* commitment alone

- *romantic love:* intimacy + passion

- *fatuous love:* passion + commitment

- *compassionate love:* commitment + intimacy

- *consummate love:* all three elements

- *non-love:* absence of all three elements.

Life and love are too messy to neatly pigeonhole into eight tidy boxes. Relationships lose their passion or shine. Even though 'complicated' may be a standard tagline for a relationship status these days, the manner in which people conduct themselves makes them far more so. If we're being inauthentic, not candid and unbending, not willing to consider how or why others act the way they do, then love becomes a damn site more complicated than it already may be. And let's be real. How many people do you know who have genuinely, bona fide, stood up in a court of law and tapped into their psychic abilities with complete, 100 per cent, accuracy?

Perhaps this is a version where all three elements of Sternberg's concept are absent. Or, more likely, someone playing out their life experiences or lower EQ. Conversely, all three elements may exist, yet a relationship may still grow apart so it's no longer consummate and where neither party is at fault. If we hold onto anger or animosity on such occasions, it may suggest the three elements initially given were only done so 'on condition'. To love unconditionally means exactly that. No expectations, no anger, if another person doesn't always deliver or act as you wish.

Martin Luther King Jnr said, 'Darkness cannot drive out darkness; only light can do that. Hate cannot drive out hate: only love can do that'.

The presence of love is far better than its absence. People often describe the opposite of love as hate. Hate is also fuelled by emotion and frequently means having less control or lower EQ. To hate, less than an ideal form, still displays a level of care factor. I've developed my own 'love triangle' theory where the three points are anchored like another school playground game. It's the relationship value equivalent of 'Rock-paper-scissors':

Hate (Fear)	trumps	Indifference
Love	beats	Hate (Fear)
Indifference	blocks	Love

Our brain's circulatory loop makes both our digital and real-world relationships similar because they are both virtual, living only inside your head. That's why digital addicts tell you to love your haters. You must be doing something right (or wrong or fake or illegal as it often turns out). No matter, it's when people are completely ignored that the imaginary pain truly hurts.

So let's now both introduce and farewell our musings on love with input from some masters. Paulo Coelho, perhaps best known for *The Alchemist* has penned many relevant works, yet lines from *By the River Piedra I Sat Down and Wept* are perhaps the most profound:

> To love is to lose control…

> Love is like a dam: if you allow a tiny crack to form through which only a trickle of water can pass, that trickle will quickly bring down the whole structure. Soon no one will be able to control the force of the current.

Rumi, the 13th century Persian poet, is one of the most celebrated writers on the subject of love. Submerging yourself in a river of his quatrains or verses, you can't help but feel awash. Perhaps though we need only ponder a single thought: 'Reason is powerless in the expression of love'.

People invest so much of their precious, tangible time to feel emotions or offer kind service. That's why no matter the layers of personal value that fuse together through life experiences as character and perceptions, there remains a common daily choice that defines you: love or fear.

Relationship value
Tools, tips and self-reflEQtion

If Dunbar, Waldinger or Rumi are to be believed, then these quick tips are aimed at tapping into a trump element! When asking people to define value I found many of them articulated value that clearly related to quality of relationship, personal interactions and personal qualities.

When drilling into these explanations, a far broader selection than the four traits of relationship value shared here are often proffered. Many may mean the same thing. Transparency, truth and honesty are all aligned with candour. Sincerity, openness, genuineness, respect and trust could just as easily be placed in the bucket of authenticity. I've honed in on four traits of relationship value I've learned are big-hitting ones that add enormous value. Choose your own if need be! Focusing on any of these will still increase feeling and add value. If other ideas spring to mind, well, you already know by now what to do: trust your instinct or initiative and take action!

Tidy up the digital you

Don't worry about what some of those fast-talking gurus or attention-seeking celebrities tell you. Fame and fortune may be nice to have but they're not paths to fulfillment. Keep the stories and ideas you share through digital as the real you. Add personal values: what do you think; what do you believe? People will appreciate the real you rather than a carbon copy wannabe.

Be more mindful of your 150

Why rush to add circles of friends. You may be adding a few stalkers or narcissists. Who are the people you're engaging with on social media? Are they really worth your precious time? Put a little more thought into who qualifies for your 'real friends' zone.

Support your 150

Once you know who your 150 are, ask how you may be able to support them. So many people will share posts, comments and testimonials for random strangers and influencers on the other side of the globe. Meanwhile friends in their inner circles, investing life savings into businesses that offer value, barely get the same support. You don't have to like or love everything. Take the time and, once in a while, if their work resonates with you, give them a little more support.

The real virtual world

I've said it before, but I'll say it again slightly differently. When you're out with friends, focus on the experience with them rather than the documentation of it. Rather than sending a text, pick up the phone. If you're going to talk on the phone for hours, which we often do anyway, then why not meet up? Think about ways to invest quality into the relationships that matter.

Random acts of kindness

Not everything we do of value has to be seen on social or even credited. Buy a coffee for the stranger next in line, put money in a parking meter: anything, no matter how trivial, delivered in kindness adds value to the world.

Resolve the unspoken and the dramas

If you've got feuds dragging on, take the high ground and be the first to speak. If you've left a trail of mess in your wake, be brave and tidy it up.If you need space, take it and then be sure to go back and talk.

If you're going to tell anyone what's bothering you, make sure it includes the people who need to hear it. Be mindful about letting annoyances become rivers and dams of bad blood. You can be candid and kind when reconciling or concluding relationships.

Have I told you lately that I love you?

Van the Man (Morrison) was onto something with this one! Not just the people you're romantically connected with. No matter where folks sit in your love triangles don't be too busy chasing fame, fortune or success to let them know you care.

6

Tying it all together

Personal and professional perspectives

Wayne Dyer famously said, 'If you change the way you look at things, the things you look at change'.

We all view things, including value, differently, so it's important to remind ourselves to adapt our approach. For example, a philosophy inspired by the Beatles—'love makes the world go round'—has been reframed as money being the primary circular cause!

Those who rank love a priority capture a perception of value, the essence of life, primarily viewed through a lens of relationship value. Those who see money as a main cause do so through the filter of tangible value.

The bigger picture is, it's all entwined:

- Perception of value is dependent on the *situation*.

- The *situation* will be linked to specific *priorities*, personal or professional.

- *Priorities*, short or long term, are made in consideration of our *values*.

- Our *values*, which may adapt, drive our decisions for *situations* or *priorities*.

And so the loop continues.

In some circumstances the priority we're facing may be immediate and viewed transactionally. Perhaps the most pressing concern is the bottom-line cost. Think about energy bills. When considering your budget for keeping your home warm you may have a sense of environment but not to the point of worrying how all the energy is harnessed, transported or delivered. Others may be happy to pay a premium amount if necessary, provided all the energy sources are considered cleaner for the environment.

Which explains the importance of governments, communities and corporates striving to achieve both goals. Sustainable, affordable energy sources, or broader solutions, make consumer decisions easier and make the world go round more harmoniously. The vitriol, be it from climate deniers or extinction rebels, would likely be far less.

The digital-age version of 'adding value' comes mostly via token social media posts packed with one-minute ideas, quotes, 'braindumps' or access to knowledge. Which is cool. If you're an influencer with a large audience you may reach tens of thousands, or millions, of connections. If you're an unknown, you may reach only a handful of people. The reach in numbers is still a measure of potential tangible value. Any social media posts or messages that are on point, researched, credible and created with powerful stories may provoke a good feeling—an emotional value. If those same messages address community or global causes, we may tap into elements of service and relationship value.

Conversely, daily social media posts can be devoid of all worth when braindumps packaged as 'thought leadership' are nothing more than selfies acting like a sugar rush. A daily fix of self-serving dopamine does little for one's own wellbeing or adding value to others. Selfies are usually about as relevant in purposeful 'value' as ice-cream mirrors or chocolate teapots.

Value and worth are neutral until they become perceived positively or negatively. As meaning-making machines we begin to anchor polarised views on the world we see.

In the early days of technology, many people loved the innovation of social media platforms. They still do. Yet that initial adoration was far less tainted with the suspicion or negativity we see today. All the values in our Value Model were more positively ticked back then: reaching vast numbers, sharing stories and innovation, promoting causes, extending connections, remaining in touch with distant family or creating new friends.

Then, as the platforms grew, people found themselves hacked, trolled or stalked more frequently. Our feeds are bombarded with fake news, rude stories, anger and hate, all of which may provoke negative tangible or emotional value. You may even find friends or connections break your trust and post personal information and stories about you without permission, eliciting a lower appreciation of the mediums through negative emotions. Fake reviews or people deliberately tearing down the efforts of others are akin to negative service value. Having to deal with online bullying, gossiping, trolling, cruelty or deceit is a simple way to view negative relationship value.

When you add to this the manner with which big data sets are harvested and leveraged for profit or politics we see a further dip in the value perception of social media platforms. Subjects such as privacy, perhaps less considered in the early days, are now at the forefront.

Information and technology may well be valuable new commodities and sources of wealth, like oil and gold, but any perceived misuse creates negative value. It's ironic that Zuckerberg's Facebook found itself having to use what it deemed as 'less valuable' billboard, print and poster advertising in order to rebuild a positive perception of value and trust!

Value disruption

During Hong Kong FinTech Week in 2018, a Russian disruptor in the banking system, Oleg Tinkov, painted a picture of how crazy the perception of value can be. Some financial tech companies are trying to create tangible value by totally eliminating fees. As Tinkov bluntly pointed out, in the manner of Cossacks taking no Napoleonic prisoners, 'Who's paying for it? Someone is. If you're not screwing the customers then you're screwing the investors!'

Capital funding investments, he cites, often become like pyramid schemes that get burned out. So many start-ups, which may have great potential, end up being 'valued' on the mere promise of the story.

Many of these start-ups never make a profit and often even run at a severe loss. In 2019 Tinkoff Bank made half a billion dollars net income in a business worth $3 billion with seven permanent establishment locations. Meanwhile, some of these 'unicorns' pop up without a single premise or asset to speak of, losing money hand over fist, some without skill or capability within the industry they're trying to disrupt, yet they find themselves valued equally at $3 billion.

Such is the power of increasing value perception in tangible, emotional, service and relationship that a dreamy whisper or the slightest suggestion of disruptive profitability leads to such lunacy. In the same way that blind faith frequently drives economies or just like guessing how many bananas one might actually have access to in the future (as in *The Laundromat*). Where an industry trends, the numbers of bananas credited to be in their future skyrockets. Sometimes these do take off.

One has been the rapid rise of e-commerce, which infiltrates virtually every industry. Statista valued the 2019 global e-commerce sales at more than US$3.5 trillion. It's estimated that the Australian market will rise to over US$25 billion by 2021 (up from US$20 billion in 2018).

As a learning and development professional, I've worked quite intensely in this space, including a stint of almost five years in Australia, New Zealand and across APAC for an early disruptor. I've inducted hundreds of employees and rolled out leadership capabilities, sales methodologies and broader business training programs across a variety of organisations.

I remember attending an inaugural APAC leadership conference where I was the only one of 40 leaders aged over 35. All were eager and bright. Some were very inexperienced or ill equipped.

It reminded me of two lines of banter from the movie *Skyfall*, where Daniel Craig's James Bond character exchanges quips when first meeting the youthful 'Q', Ben Whishaw, in a museum gallery:

'Age is no guarantee of efficiency.'

'And youth is no guarantee of innovation.'

Both are true. Yet as we all know, as every generation ultimately learns, the passage of time creates greater personal value through incorporating learnings from life experiences.

Even the smartest 16 or 26 year old will likely look back when they are 36, 46, 56 or beyond and realise how naive they once were. Or how much they've since grown. I know that if I were to develop leaders now for Contiki, my efforts would be more sophisticated given my additional two decades of knowledge as a professional.

Some emerging industries feel like a revolving door of talent rather than a consolidation of opportunity. There's a race to be perceived as successful rather than an effort to incorporate values or behaviour to add true value to others.

In my 10 years with Contiki the rotation of senior leader stakeholders I had to partner with included one CEO, three GMs and three operational heads. One of them, to this day, remains the only person in my life I'll affectionately refer to as the 'boss' (thanks, Jo, for setting me on my path in development!). Some of the broader network of key stakeholders—for example, a small group of loyal independent Italian business owners and collaborators collectively and affectionately known as 'The Florentines'—have been held in high esteem at Contiki for literally decades because of their diligence and the manner in which they treat others.

Conversely, in four and a half years of experience establishing learning and development frameworks with one organisation in Australia, the rotation of key stakeholders included three CEOs, four COOs, five CFOs, six heads of sales and close to 50 managers, inducting almost 500 employees in the process. All for a business with circa 150 (Dunbar's number!) as a stable headcount.

The nature of disruptive business encourages people to desire rapid personal success or to be perceived as a personal brand in their own right. I've had people ask how I got to my level, skill or knowledge within my field. They fail to realise that what they're trying to shortcut—life experience and time—is the key. You can accelerate it by conscious effort and being more present. You can't shortcut it.

We live in an era where we're frequently told titles are no longer of value or no longer matter. That's not true. If it were, why are so many people eager to label themselves as entrepreneurs, disruptors, innovators, founders, directors, motivational speakers, celebrities, media personalities or CEOs? In fact, it's just that the new generation values different titles. Sometimes they'll go as far as creating a great-sounding one that makes you wonder what the person's responsibility actually is.

For example a founder of an organisation claiming to disrupt marketing may call themselves 'Chief Wizard of Lightbulb Moments'. In reality this is a first-year marketing degree student charging their parents' friends $10 a week to put together a few social media ads as a side hustle. The drive is noble. The brag in title or achievement is perhaps a little premature.

Some of the most innovative leaders I've worked with have been within digital industries—whether disruptive or not. Others may well have been armed with excessive hubris yet their lack of worldly experience or willingness to learn, along with rushing to get ahead, means they frequently miss the value mark. This aggressive pace is part of the challenge of valuing people or adding value.

I've seen businesses make high-volume sales, only to find themselves refunding half due to poor customer experiences, a lack of sustainable processes or a limited appreciation of end-user value. One of the most valuable things you can do is slow down and build personal skills or a business culture where value is truly understood and applied by all.

Harvard Business Review summarises the economies evolution well:

- *agrarian economy*: make a cake yourself from scratch with raw ingredients at a base cost

- *goods economy*: buy some pre-packaged ingredients for ease for a few extra dollars

- *service economy*: have other specialists make the cake for you for 10–15 times the raw cost of goods

- *experience economy*: package total memorable events where the cake is a small part and likely thrown in for free!

You can see the same evolution extrapolated in an industry like travel: local holidays, packaged holidays, specialist agents organising everything, or trips and tours with bundled excursions and experiences galore.

Qualtrics, a leading experience management company, highlights the four primary experiences a business may focus on as:

- customer experience

- employee experience

- product experience
- brand experience.

This means building a playbook that adds real value through multiple mechanisms. Many tips in this book would qualify. Make sure to measure typical operational data (tangible value data) and also capture experiential data (typically born from soft skills associated with the other value model components—emotional value, service value and relationship value) to achieve the desired nirvana, namely turning:

- customers into evangelists
- employees into ambassadors
- products into obsessions
- brands into icons.

Working at Contiki gave me exposure to industries classically related to our more ancient hardwired technology: human connection and human touch. As you've seen, industries like tourism, travel, hospitality and retail inherently taught me many of the practical ideas laid out in my Value Model.

Angels and demons

Some industries are being demonised because their market approach is guided by the tangible value linked to greed—pharmaceuticals is an example.

In the early 2000s Valeant Pharmaceuticals (now Bausch Health) began a strategic spree of mergers and acquisitions, essentially buying out pharmaceutical companies, then stripping the research and development allocated budgets (often about 18 per cent) down to about 3 per cent. After acquisition, they targeted a campaign of jacking up prices without any improvement or change to the existing—often long established—drugs.

Syprene is a vital drug for the survival of approximately one in 30 000 people of the population who are affected by Wilson's disease—an inability to process copper—which is fatal if left untreated. The price for Syprene skyrocketed from about $400 a year to about $289 000.

Valeant did the same with dozens, if not hundreds, of drugs using the strategy of predatory pricing or by creating alliances or ownership of dodgy suburban pharmacies whose primary purpose was to milk high quantities of money for drug payments through insurance companies.

This level of corporate avarice elevated Valeant's valuation from $2.3 billion to as high as $79 billion. Chairman and CEO Michael Pearson revealed all when describing his job: 'to create shareholder value'. Perhaps so, but not at any price. And certainly not at the expense of ethics or morals, both of which are intrinsically linked to the etymology of the word value.

Former hedge fund manager Martin Shkreli is potentially the individual devil child of such greed. He was, at one time, 'the most hated man in America' after increasing the price of the antiparasitic drug Daraprim from $13.50 per pill to $750. He was charged, and Senators scorned Shkreli during hearings for his constant inappropriate courtroom smirk. The situation wasn't funny given people were dying. Shkreli no doubt lost his smug smile after swapping grey tailored suits for an orange federal prison jumpsuit when sentenced to seven years in jail in 2018.

Let it serve as a warning. When you rush your dealings with others and exclude building an authentic, considerate relationship with them; or disregard the importance of delivering experiences that provoke positive emotions; or neglect to engage people's senses; or when quality service is traded to treat people like cash cows, you will lose contacts and customers. Greed will lose you value in this modern era of human connection blended with the digital age.

Tattoo 'adding value' into your ethos

Contiki has thrived as a brand since 1961. People even tattoo its brand or symbolic hashtag (#noregrets) on their bodies as a souvenir of the experience! Harley Davidson tribe members do the same. When you deliver an experience that makes people literally want to scar their body for life you must be delivering a feeling of exceptional value—so you should strive to add and deliver value through personal interactions, products, services and experiences.

As Steve Jobs once alluded, make your products or service so good that people want to lick them!

If Contiki can encourage permanent skin branding, then other companies could assuredly deliver value encouraging additional ink studio visits from their own tribe. (Nike's '#justdoit' would tuck neatly onto a bicep or calf.)

The best ideas or solutions aren't always the ones that gain traction. They just may miss the mark. They blunder or fall short, tapping into multiple aspects of the value perception psyche, or they fail to spike a high appeal to blatantly obvious filters most suitable for some experiences. How we conduct ourselves and our ability to educate and demonstrate value to others is on us. We live in a noisy world. More doesn't necessarily make you stand out. Quality does.

We've already seen in the current digital age that, unfortunately, the polarity may at times be true. It's amazing what some people get away with for a while. (Think Elizabeth Holmes or Belle Gibson.) We can see they do so by leveraging values powerfully on their ego ride — often by accident, slipping habitually to ones that are default or perceptions in their own skills or approach. The five values laid out in this book—each with its four primary layers—will help you better understand what some of the more significant ones are.

Let me be clear that, even in writing the book, I also remain a learner. This is true for any venture. Identifying significant factors doesn't mean I've personally mastered them all. For me the component of tangible value has potentially, personally, been an Achilles heel, as I shared earlier. I'm a little like PIXAR in my approach to life: the drive to deliver creativity and build meaningful relationship means I'm not always as laser focused or as objectively considered when it comes to important themes like cash flow. My personal quest to add value, especially in consideration of other people, means any notion of a budget is a good suggestion rather than a necessity. I still need to work on this.

There are times in my life where Warren Buffet's idea that 'if you buy things you do not need, soon you will have to sell the things you need' was written personally for me. Tailored suits. Oh dear.

Mind you, at least I'm glad I'm not on the other side of that equation, the greed side, where I'd adapt Warren Buffet's perspective: if you fail to focus on service, emotional or relationship value for the sake of tangible value results, soon you'll find results will fail abysmally until you focus on them all.

Strive to add value outside of the product, service or goods exchange. People frequently elevate in value the unexpected things you do for them. The surprises, the value added extras, are often the things they value the most.

In the introduction I shared a view that if a human being were a land mass, value is a combination of the well that rises within and the ocean that surrounds and continually massages us in tides. In the modern age the continual evolution, innovation and impact of technology forms a significant part of those external waves.

We know that water is the universal symbol for emotion and feeling. What we also know about water and waves, from

Buddhist meditation philosophies, is they can't be held back, nor can they be prevented from disintegrating. Waves, good or bad, are impermanent. Fulfillment comes when you can appreciate and ride the good waves and not worry about the bad ones.

If you read books like *Sapiens* by Yuval Noah Harari, you may accept it's inevitable that as a species we'll continue to evolve where technology and science are a core part of our transformation. They can't be disregarded as part of our new value systems or values. He surmises that 'an insignificant animal minding its own business in a corner of Africa…transformed itself into the master of the entire planet and the terror of the eco system'. Poised at a critical juncture of human history, one of the ultimate questions is posed, 'What do we want to become now?'

We're colliding into one another, making accords with one another and coexisting in environments, communities and relationships. We navigate dealings both personal and professional that are business transactions and social ones. The way you can better affect, build or improve value is through a conscious ability to identify or differentiate your own favoured filters, and then adapt. If you find yourself unable to identify the unique manner in which others may perceive their world, you now have my Value Model to focus on. Fill all the value buckets as much as possible with consistency.

Epilogue:
Aristotle to Audrey

From the father of philosophy to the divine feminine

My inspiration for this Value Model of five values with four layers each may well have come from the father of philosophy, yet Aristotle, like all humans, wasn't without flaws. He lived in different times. A few of his ideals would equally relegate his space on the pedestal amid important values in our modern times.

Multiple historians cite Aristotle as having counselled Alexander the Great to be 'a leader to the Greeks and a despot to the Barbarians' when describing how the warrior king might treat defeated tribes. Aristotle argued that slaves had an inherent slavish nature. Believing that others are only good for a life of servitude and slavery beneath you doesn't bode well. It's quite the antithesis of emotional, service and relationship value!

But that doesn't take away from ideas like potentiality and actuality, those five values or the realisation they were intertwined.

When I first released content for this model into the public arena it was for the inaugural TEDxCasey event. Good curation for TED events is important and content has to be aligned with any overarching theme, in this instance it was 'two hands'. As soon as I heard the theme, one person sprang to mind.

Audrey Hepburn was born in Brussels. She spent her childhood in the lowlands of Europe and England. The American Film Institute ranked her the third greatest screen legend of all time, coming in behind Katherine Hepburn and Bette Davis, which places her in great company and fine standing.

It's also a testament to her enduring divine and enchanting presence that in 1955, despite not starring in any new films that year, she still picked up the Golden Globe Film Favorite award. It's also kind of perfect that in her final starring role, in the Steven Spielberg movie *Always* alongside Richard Dreyfuss, she plays a role akin to a guardian angel.

Far more appealing than her celebrity, beyond acting capabilities or as a fashion icon in the golden age of Hollywood, were her perspectives and philosophies on living a happy life. Audrey Hepburn dedicated much of her time to humanitarian work, especially in her later years, to organisations such as UNICEF.

As an epitome of style, class, grace, love and good taste, I'm sure spending even 15 minutes over a coffee with her, if not the full breakfast at Tiffany's, one might have learned to ignite the heart and mind. It's no surprise that her legend and legacy remain.

And it was Audrey Hepburn who said, 'As you grow older you will discover you have two hands: one for helping yourself, the other for helping others'.

A definition of value

'Define value for me.'

We come full circle back to the question that began this journey. I'm going to answer it now in a couple of ways. They're perhaps less ambiguous and more practical to apply than the definition 'perception or regard that something is held to deserve' that you'll find in the dictionary.

These holistic explanations are a combination of my own experiences in addition to other credible ideas and studies. Definitions leaving fewer, if any, gaps lurking in dark corners of the mind.

First let me adapt Miss Hepburn's beautiful words. Consider that a way to add real value is to appeal to both the head and the heart and use those two hands, along with the rest of you, to be of service to your community.

A more practical way to define value is combining and appreciating all five values of the Value Model:

- *Personal value*: leverage your strengths, identify your motivation, apply EQ with an open mindset and look for clues in others

- *Tangible value*: show me the evidence, benchmark and prove it through the four fundamental layers: dollars, percentages, numbers and time

- *Emotional value*: master stories; tell great stories, ignite and engage my senses, personalise things, make me feel it and strive to spark a 'wow!'

- *Service value*: act upon positively thought-out long-term solutions enriching the lives of others and simultaneously respecting the environment

- *Relationship value*: be candid and authentic as the best version of yourself with dollops of kindness and love in everything you do.

There are questions you can learn to ask yourself:

- Which elements of value do I tend to bias or lean towards?

- Which are less appealing; which may be important to others?

- What are the clues I can look for or pick up so I might adapt?

- Which tips or ideas might I want to experiment with and adapt?

The thing I've found most curious through my journey is the etymology of the word 'value' itself. Its roots are in the Latin, *valere*, and Middle English, and then adapted from old French, *valoir*.

If everyone acted to add value by heeding the original definition, our world would bode well. And that definition is:

Value: to be of worth, moral worth.

Albert Einstein summed it all up beautifully when he said, 'Strive not to be a person of success but rather to be a person of value'.

The Add Value
nursery rhyme

How, why, do and who
Are four primary layers contributing to the total sum of you
Amidst the mix live both true values and your perception of value

Dollars, percentage, numbers and time
Is the tangible value nursery rhyme
But the metrics that matter are yours, not mine!

Story, senses, personal and unique, like wow
To tap into emotional value, these are the four ways how
Then add a touch of creativity for that extra reooooww!

Service to others is the rent we all pay
Focus on solutions + possibilities, others + environment every day
The trick's to not let short-term thinking or gains get in the way

Add Value

For relationship ace traits, choose your own if you must

But be candid and brave with two common languages: kindness and love

For quality character and value fit together, like two hands in gloves.

MC

References

Adventures of Andre and Wally B, 1984. The Graphics Group, Pixar.

Always, 1989. Steven Spielberg, Universal Pictures, United Artists, Amblin Entertainment.

Babiak, P & Hare, RD 2006. *Snakes in Suits*, Harper Business.

Belic, R 2011. *Happy*, Wadi Rum Productions.

Besson, L 1997. *The Fifth Element*, Columbia Pictures.

Binet, A 1905. 'The Mind and the Brain': 'L'Etude Experimentale de L'intelligence'.

Brown, B 2011. *Power of Vulnerability* [Video recording] TED.

Butler, O 2019. *How to Bullshit Your Way to Number 1*, Where Publications.

Campbell, J 2004. 'Follow your Bliss' theory, *Pathways to Bliss*, The Joseph Campbell Foundation.

Carter, M 2017. *Ignite Your Potential*, self-published.

Citizen Kane, 1941. Orson Welles, RKO Pictures.

Coelho, P 2004. *7th Day Trilogy*, Harper Collins.

Coelho, P 2006. *By the River Piedra I Sat Down and Wept*, Harper One.

Coleman, D 1996. *Emotional Intelligence*, Bloomsbury.

Courtney, B 1998. *Recipe for Dreaming*, Penguin Australia.

Csikszentmihalyi, M 2000. *Beyond Boredom and Anxiety*, Jossey-Bass.

Csikszentmihalyi, M 2003. *Good Business*, Hodder and Stoughton.

Dirty Money, 2018. Episode 3: 'Drug Short', Erin Lee Carr, Netflix.

Dreary, T 1994. *Horrible Histories: The Rotten Romans*, Scholastic.

Dreary, T 2004. *France (Horrible Histories Special)*, Gardners Books.

Dunant, H 1862. *A Memory of Solferino*, The International Committee Of The Red Cross.

Dunbar, R 2012. *Can the Internet Buy You More Friends?* [Video recording] TED.

Dyer, W 2006. *The Secrets of an Inspirational (in Spirit) Life*, Hay House.

Empodocles, original theory of the four classical elements.

Falcon, A 2019. 'Aristotle on Causality', *Stanford Encyclopedia of Philosophy*.

Forrest Gump 1994. Robert Zemeckis, Paramount Pictures. Based on the 1986 novel by Winston Groom.

Gates, W 2010. *Innovating to Zero.* [Video recording] TED.

Gilbert, D 2014. *The Surprising Science of Happiness.* [Video recording] TED.

Gladiator 2000. Ridley Scott, Universal Pictures.

Harry Potter and the Order of the Phoenix 2007. David Yates Warner Brothers.

Hicks, E & Hicks, J 2006. *Ask and It's Given*, Hay House Australia.

'Hiroshima': *BBC History of World War II*, 2005. Paul Wilmshurst, distributed by BBC.

Inside Bill's Brain 2019. Davis Guggenheim, Netflix.

Inside Job 2010. Charles Ferguson, Sony Pictures Classics.

Investopedia. [Website] https://www.investopedia.com/

Jerry McGuire 1996. Cameron Crowe and James L Brooks, TriStar Pictures.

Joachim, HH 1930. 'Aristotle, on Generation and Corruption' in WD Ross, *The Works of Aristotle*, vol. 2, Oxford.

Joachim, HH 1930. 'Aristotle's Model of Four Causes': Le Moyne College Notes, *On Generation and Corruption*, in WD Ross 1930, *The Works of Aristotle*, vol. 2, Oxford.

Jung, C 1971. *Psychological Types*, Kingston University Press.

Kipling, R 1910. *If*, Doubleday, Page & Companies.

Kiyosaki, R 1997. *Rich Dad, Poor Dad*, Plata Publishing.

Kübler-Ross, E 1969. *On Death and Dying*, Macmillan Company.

Maslow, A 1954. *Motivation and Personality*, Harper & Brothers.

McGregor, D 2006. *The Human Side of Enterprise*, McGraw-Hill Education.

Michelin 1994. *Green Guide Paris*, John Murray.

Michelin 1994. *Green Guide France*, 2nd edn.

Moulton Marston, W 1938. *Emotions of Normal People*, Richard Smith.

Myers–Briggs, 1998. *MBTI Manual*, 3rd edn, CPP.

Pevsner, J 2019. 'Leonardo da Vinci's Studies of the Brain', *Lancet*, 6 April, pp. 1465–72.

Pine, J & Gilmore, J 1998. 'Welcome to the experience economy', *Harvard Business Review*, July–August.

Pink, D 2011. *Drive*, Canongate.

Pratchett, T. 'Discworld' series, Transworld Publishers, Doubleday.

Rauscher, FH, Shaw, GL, Ky, KN 1993. Music and spatial task performance. Nature, 'Mozart effect', *Journal of Royal Society of Medicine*, 365, 611.

Sinek, S 2014. *How Great Leaders Inspire Action*. [Video recording] TED.

Spranger, E 1928. *Types of Men: The Psychology and Ethics of Personality*, M Niemeyer in Halle (Saale).

Stanford Binet Testing Scores. Overviews, general guides.

Sternberg, RJ 1988. *Triangle of Love*, Basic Books.

Stone, I 1961. *The Agony and the Ecstasy*, Doubleday.

The Inventor: Out for Blood in Silicon Valley, 2019. Gibney, HBO.

The Laundromat 2019. Steven Soderbergh, Netflix.

The Pursuit 2019. John Papola, Samuel Goldwyn Films / Amazon Prime.

The Roosevelts: An Intimate History 2014. Ken Burns, PBS.

The Teddy Bear Shop Melbourne, Steiff Bears for Live TEDx Casey event plus additional insights, Margarete Steiff.

Waldinger, R 2017/2018. *What Makes a Good Life*. [Video recording] TED. https://singjupost.com/robert-waldinger-on-the-good-life-at-tedxbeaconstreet-full-transcript/2/

Ware, L 2000. *The Guardian* obituary 17 August.

Welch, J 2005. *Winning*, Harper Business.

Zunin, L 1972. *Contact: The First Four Minutes*, Ballantine Books.

Index

21982319691154

CPSIA information can be obtained
at www.ICGtesting.com
Printed in the USA
BVHW040808180920
588896BV00032B/98

9 780730 384021